Money *Diaries*

with She's *on the* Money

Victoria Devine has transformed the way young people think about money. With a background in behavioural psychology, Victoria knows how to make hard-to-understand concepts fun, fresh and relatable, sharing her wisdom through her chart-topping podcast *She's on the Money*, several bestselling books on money and a regular finance column in *The Age* and *Sydney Morning Herald*.

Now retired from her role as a financial adviser, Victoria is a co-director and founder of Zella Money, an award-winning mortgage-broking business, while continuing to provide financial education through her She's on the Money platform, tools and website. She has been a guest speaker at events and featured in publications such as *Financial Standard*, *Vogue*, ABC News, RMIT Future of Financial Planning, Mamamia, *Elle* magazine, Yahoo Finance and many more. She was also named on the *Forbes* 30 Under 30 Asia list for 2021.

Victoria's number one bestselling first book, *She's on the Money*, won the ABIA General Non-fiction Book of the Year 2022 and the Best Personal Finance & Investment Book of the Year at the 2021 Business Book Awards.

shesonthemoney.com.au

@shesonthemoneyaus

@ShesontheMoneyAUS

Also by Victoria Devine

She's on the Money
Investing with She's on the Money
She's on the Money Budget Journal
Property with She's on the Money

Money *Diaries*

with She's *on the* Money

The power in rewriting your money story

Victoria Devine

LIFE

PENGUIN LIFE

UK | USA | Canada | Ireland | Australia
India | New Zealand | South Africa | China

Penguin Life is part of the Penguin Random House group of companies
whose addresses can be found at global.penguinrandomhouse.com

Penguin Random House Australia

First published by Penguin Life in 2024

Cover design by Alissa Dinallo © Penguin Random House Australia Pty Ltd
Text design by Alissa Dinallo and Post Pre-Press Group, Australia
Author photograph by Miranda Stokke
Typeset in 10.5/14 pt Mercury Text by Post Pre-press Group, Australia

Printed and bound in Australia by Griffin Press, an accredited
ISO AS/NZS 14001 Environmental Management Systems printer

NATIONAL LIBRARY OF AUSTRALIA

A catalogue record for this book is available from the National Library of Australia

ISBN 978 1 76134 771 9

penguin.com.au

FSC www.fsc.org
MIX
Paper | Supporting responsible forestry
FSC® C018684

We at Penguin Random House Australia acknowledge that Aboriginal and Torres Strait Islander peoples are the Traditional Custodians and the first storytellers of the lands on which we live and work. We honour Aboriginal and Torres Strait Islander peoples' continuous connection to Country, waters, skies and communities. We celebrate Aboriginal and Torres Strait Islander stories, traditions and living cultures; and we pay our respects to Elders past and present.

As the author of this book I'd like to acknowledge and pay respect to Australia's Aboriginal and Torres Strait Islander peoples, the traditional custodians of lands, waterways and skies across Australia. I'd like to particularly acknowledge the Wurundjeri people of the Kulin Nation who are the traditional custodians of the land on which I was able to write this book. I pay my respects to Elders past and present, and I share my friendship and kindness.

For *you*! I am so proud of your journey thus far and I can't wait to see where your story takes you next.

Contents

Introduction

Hello, my friend! I'm so glad you've picked up my book and decided it was interesting enough to open it up and start reading! If we've met before, you already know that I consider the Money Diaries a treasured part of the *She's on the Money* podcast. I'm over the moon to have curated some of my all-time favourites (plus a few brand-new ones here, especially for you!) into a book you can hold and share and talk about.

If, by chance, we haven't yet crossed paths – hello, my newest friend. I'm Victoria Devine, your neuro-spicy, animal-loving finance expert and I'm absolutely thrilled you're here. I'm a Melbourne-based millennial, new mum (!), retired financial adviser, Managing Director of Zella Money (the best mortgage broking team in Australia, if you ask me), and the voice and brains behind *She's on the Money* – Australia's number one business and finance podcast.

Money is something I'm wildly passionate about and I'm especially passionate about empowering women to not only become financially literate, but financially free. When one of us rises, we all rise – and the world becomes a better place. Sharing our stories is ingrained in the She's on the Money community and is one of the things I love most about us, so let me share a few things about me before you jump into the juicy money stories you're here for.

I'm not someone who's always been good with money. In fact, I used to be pretty terrible at it before I fell into the finance space. I got a credit card at the ripe old age of 18 which spiralled into more than $40,000 worth of personal debt that I had to crawl my way out of. Do I regret it, though? No, not really – because that journey is what led me here, to you. And now, I'm in the very special position of leading the She's on the Money community and helping women every single day to take control of their finances, change their money stories and start investing in their future selves. So if anyone knows how impactful a money story is, it's definitely me.

I've curated this book to be an engaging, exciting and inspiring set of stories that'll help you see that it's completely possible to change the trajectory of your life. Money stories are far more important than you might initially think. Whether we like it or not, these subconscious and conscious thoughts, values, beliefs and behaviours we hold to be true about money direct how our money story plays out in our future, unless we take control. And that's exactly why I've written this book – so you can be empowered by your money story, rather than overwhelmed, and hopefully start to see that every single one of us has the agency to change our lives for the better.

While many people in our community have transformed their money stories to create abundance, plenty of others are still feeling totally lost about their finances and wondering if they can ever create the life they want to live. Spoiler alert: you absolutely can, and, my friend – I *know* you will. The diaries that have so very generously been shared with us in this book are like a giant neon sign saying, *Hey, you! No matter where you're from or what your financial past looks like, you have the power to rewrite your story!*

In this book, you will experience 25 authentic, honest and inspiring money stories covering topics as broad as work, lifestyle, property, mindset and debt. I'm sure you'll relate to many aspects of these narratives – and if you can't, perhaps you're the perfect diarist for me to feature in the next edition of this book! These stories are powerful testimonies proving that regardless of your background or past relationship with money, taking back financial control is possible for everyone. I am so honoured by the willingness of these beautiful members of my community to open up and share their journeys. Their stories not only provide valuable insights, but also offer an opportunity for each of us to learn and benefit from their experiences. A big motivation for me in creating the Money Diaries podcast segment, and now this book, has been to create the space for women to talk candidly about money – their fears, triumphs and lessons – to make it less of a 'taboo' subject. It's a big part of life, so it seems crazy to me not to discuss it openly!

There are so many incredible people I've had the privilege of speaking with to put this book together. Our diarists include those who've navigated serious challenges such as homelessness, single parenting and redundancy, others who've scored lottery wins or inheritances or built impressive side hustles, to those who've overcome the trauma of having their house burn down, being scammed by their own family and escaping coercive control. Trust me, friends, this book is juicier than you'd ever expect a money book to be!

The one thing all these stories have in common, which resonates with all of us, is that money impacts everyone, irrespective of your background and where you've come from. Each story speaks to the shared struggles and successes that we all experience on our financial journeys. They are proof that we can break free from inherited patterns and decide the direction for our own lives. The key lies in cultivating self-awareness, embracing continuous self-learning and exercising the discipline needed for change.

A huge part of the positive effect of sharing our money stories is the insight we gain through speaking them out loud and/or writing them down. Expressing them allows us to see our stories through a fresh lens, offering a perspective on them that we may never have had before. That's why I'll often ask our money diarists, both at the beginning of our chats and then again at the end, what grade they would give their money habits. It's amazing what new insights arise once we've spent some time reflecting on our subconscious beliefs and behaviours! This awareness can often be the catalyst for resetting our path and getting us closer to our future financial dreams.

So, in this book I've included thought-provoking journalling prompts to help you reflect on your own money story, so you can better understand its impact on your behaviour and reshape your mindset to gain greater financial control over your life. Throughout the stories I've also added some tips and suggestions that may help if you find yourself in similar circumstances to our diarists. And, finally, I've included many money-saving tips from the incredible She's on the Money community to help inspire us all! These gems are designed to help you spark ideas and pocket a little extra cash, because who doesn't love a good money win, right?

This book means so much to me and is arguably my favourite one to date. I genuinely believe that by sharing these stories the world is going to be in a far better place. It is my hope that these pages give you permission to rewrite your own money story and redefine your future – you deserve it and future you is going to thank you!

Lots of love, Victoria x

THINKING ABOUT YOUR MONEY STORY

This book is a collection of twenty of my favourite interviews from the Money Diaries segment of my podcast *She's on the Money* plus five all-new, exclusive ones. Each week I interview someone from our community prompting them to share their unique money story, based on this list of questions:

- What grade would you give your money habits from A to F?
- What's your attitude towards money?
- What do you do for work and how much do you earn?
- What is your big money goal?
- Do you have investments?
- Do you have debts?
- What is your best money habit?
- What is your worst money habit?
- Now that we've spoken today, what grade would you give your money habits from A to F?

The ways in which your money beliefs affect your prosperity lies at the heart of what we teach at She's on the Money. As you read along, our diarists' stories might prompt you to question your own money mindset. The first chapter of my first book, *She's on the Money*, focuses solely on this and includes an activity called Connecting With Your Money Story, to help you understand your own money story more deeply. I've also included it in the back of this book if you'd like to work through it now. Otherwise, the prompts on the next page are a good place to start.

In short, while we often inherit our money story as a subconscious belief system, once we start to become aware of the thoughts that drive our behaviours, we find ourselves in the powerful position of being able to change them. Throughout this book I offer journalling prompts to encourage you to think about your own money story and reflect on how you might respond in various scenarios.

What beliefs around money have you inherited from your upbringing: family, school and society? Some common ones are:

Money doesn't grow on trees.

Money is the root of all evil.

We'll always be broke.

Money doesn't last.

....

....

....

....

....

....

How might these core beliefs be affecting your money habits and situation?

For example, if you believe that money is a constant struggle you may find yourself feeling constantly under financial pressure, even when receiving regular pay rises – perhaps unconsciously increasing your spending habits each time your salary increases.

....

....

....

....

....

....

What new beliefs could you create that offer a more positive outlook? Ideas such as:

There's more than enough money to go around.

Hard work pays off.

The more I teach myself about money, the wealthier I become.

I get paid well for my contributions.

Mindset

From start to finish, your money mindset makes a huge difference to your financial end result. We all face real-world challenges, but there's no denying that your attitude affects your actions. If you act from a place of scarcity you'll never believe you're worthy of wealth and may find yourself engaging in self-defeating behaviours, whereas if you believe in abundance you'll tend to attract and capitalise on opportunities that take you to the next level.

Rather than playing small and remaining victims of circumstance, our community's money legends take proactive steps towards realising their best financial future by showing a willingness to examine their money mindset and transform it into their most powerful asset. I hope through hearing their stories, you're inspired to do the same!

A Breath of Fresh Air

This money diarist grew up with a single dad who worked long hours to make ends meet, but unfortunately despite that, got into a heap of debt. Luckily, with help from a supportive aunt our diarist improved her financial position and, at just 28, has bought a home and is planning a wedding, all while building her future wealth. Go, queen!

If I asked you to give your money habits a grade from A through to F, what would it be?

I think I'm probably a B minus. I've been able to work out my finances pretty well, but I still have a lot to learn. I haven't really jumped into the investing space and I'm not really ready to yet, so I want to learn more about that and build more wealth that way.

Tell us a little bit more about your money story.

My parents split up when I was eight and my dad was given custody of my brother and me. My dad had to work really, really crazy hours – from 4 am till 6 pm most days – to earn enough money to support us. I did a lot of the housework and would have dinner on the table ready when he came home. From a pretty young age, I did all the things a mother would usually do. My dad got made redundant twice in three years and got into about $40,000 worth of debt. It wasn't like he was out buying flashy things or anything like that. He just spent to keep us in school and buy the essentials we needed.

He really looked after us as best as he could and every weekend we'd do an activity – we'd go to Timezone or we'd go ice skating or rock climbing – but there wasn't an endless flow of money. I grew up with the mindset that if you work hard it'll pay off and you'll get somewhere in life. I got my first job at 14 and I was helping Dad out with the rent from 16 onwards and that taught me a lot about money and what I wanted for my future and for my own family. I didn't want my kids to grow up like that. Seeing what my dad went through, I've worked really hard to build a better foundation for myself.

What's it like being 16 and contributing to the rent when I'm assuming a lot of your peers were in a completely different position?

Pretty much all my friends' parents were together. They hadn't been through what I'd been through. I'm very close with my dad, so I was happy to help out. It started off as just $50 a week and gradually went up from there, but I was just happy to help because I knew how much he was sacrificing for us.

Is it something you talked about at school with your friends?

Not really. My friends and I all worked at the local McDonald's, but they were working to have their own money to buy themselves stuff whereas I was working to help with the bills. I was also paying off my own phone and saving for my very first car. I've never had help, so I don't think I really spoke about it in that sense with my friends at the time.

Working at McDonald's is such a good job because it's so structured and provides so much leadership training.

Definitely. It was a great place for me to start. I spent five years there and worked my way up. I started the management program but didn't finish it. Eventually, I wanted to move on, but McDonald's instilled a lot in me and it's a great starting point for teenagers; it teaches you a lot. When I began work there, I was the shyest person you'd ever meet. My dad laughs about it now, how shy I was. I wouldn't even go up to a checkout person and ask a question! People who know me now think I'm a foghorn. I make friends everywhere.

So what do you do for work now? And how much do you earn?

I work as an accounts and admin clerk. My salary is $56,000 plus super, but I also get monthly overtime and I began doing Uber Eats at the end of last year to help pay off my wedding. All my Uber Eats income goes straight to the wedding budget and then my normal salary covers the mortgage and bills and that sort of stuff.

An accounts clerk is not usually a role where you'd get overtime. How did that happen?

I work in the automotive industry, so we work on a monthly basis. At the end of each month we have to get everything entered into the system. So, generally, the last two days of the month we work 12- to 13-hour days. At the end of the month it's always really work-heavy and the start of the month's usually quiet. At the end of every month I get, maybe, $400 or $500 worth of overtime. I put my overtime funds into my wedding dress account – the money for the dress doesn't come out of my normal salary. I've set a budget for my wedding dress and don't want to spend more than about $2500.

Wedding dresses can be crazy expensive, right?!

Yeah, but I've set a very strict budget. I've run the numbers multiple times and gotten quotes for everything and I have everything structured.

What about your overall budget for your wedding? Did you and your partner work that out together?

If I turned around tomorrow and said, let's just have a party, he'd be happy with that. He definitely wants a wedding, but he finds the costs insane and we aren't made of money. So he's more about, we can have a wedding but we're not going to be able to have all the bells and whistles, so we need to be smart about it. He doesn't think spending a huge amount of money on it when we could go overseas instead is smart.

So we looked at venues and came to a number of $25,000 for everything. I'm sitting a little bit under that at the moment. We've set a date and we've booked the venue. So yeah, I'm comfortable that amount is reasonable. I think if it went over that just for our personal goals, it would be too much. We try to work out what our goals are and what's reasonable.

She's *on the* Money

I always talk about needing to check your values with your partner when it comes to the wedding spend, so you're on the same page. But that includes your family and bridesmaids and groomsmen too. You don't want your perfect day to be tinged with other people's discomfort or resentment.

Until I became a bride, I hadn't thought much about the impact of wedding costs. When I was a bridesmaid, I was at an age where I had free cashflow, so I was happy to pay for things. But when it came to my own wedding, I hated the idea that my tastes could end up putting my friends out.

With everything we might expect our bridesmaids to pay for – the hen's party and then a specific pair of shoes and dress, or their own hair and makeup – it all adds up. If you ask them to pay for it, you might be impacting their ability to take a holiday, or to help their mum or to reach their own financial goals.

I put myself in their shoes: if I was asked to be a bridesmaid today, would I have the funds to go and spend that amount? With my money goals at the moment, would that be a priority for me? And in that moment I realised I didn't want my wedding to be someone else's financial burden.

Are you paying for your bridesmaids and what led you to your decision?

I was always planning to pay for their hair and make-up, and originally thought that they would buy their own dresses and that I'd buy their shoes – unless they already have some that fit the colour scheme, then I'm happy for them to wear what they have. I'd love to be able to afford to pay for everything and the way I'm working things out now, I should be able to pay at least half, if not all.

Alright, I want to know, apart from the wedding on the horizon, what are your other big money goals?

After the wedding we want to build our emergency funds. We've set up a bank account named 'emergency funds', but it's yet to have any money put in it. I want to build a buffer for our mortgage repayments. I'm lucky in that my auntie is a mortgage broker. She looks over my finances 24/7 and since I was 14 I've been asking her those sorts of questions. She's really helped guide me finance-wise, helping me when I have to make big decisions and advising me how to structure things.

How fantastic having an aunt who's a mortgage broker! It sounds like you have really clear goals and ideas of cashflow and budgeting. Did you find out about it from your aunt? How did you learn about money?

It came partly from seeing my dad struggle and then partly from my auntie being in the finance industry. My auntie and I had a lot of conversations about money. From the day I got my first job I used to write on a notepad how much I got paid each week and what my bills were or what my expenses were. Since the day I got my very first paycheque, I've written out my budget and still do to this day. I like putting pen to paper; seeing things written down. My auntie definitely helped with navigating how I work out my finances, so from day one I've taken responsibility. I paid for my very first car at age 17 and that was something I had to budget for as a 16 year old. I've always had money goals or something I was saving for and I knew that the only way to save or get there was to budget for it.

Is this something that your aunt just sat you down and told you, or were you tenacious in asking these sorts of questions?

My auntie took on a bit of a mothering role when my parents split up. She doesn't have children of her own, so when my parents split, my brother and I lived with her for a while as we weren't allowed to be at our old family house at the time. My auntie and I had this tradition when I was still in school that we'd have breakfast every week. I'd also have dinner with her every Sunday and we'd talk about what my financial goals were and what I was working towards. So it was a bit of both – me asking questions and her giving advice. When I got my first $30,000 loan, I didn't tell her and she was not impressed!

As a mortgage broker, she would've been a little bit salty on you, my friend!

Yeah, I got in a bit of trouble for that. But I go to her with anything when it comes to money or big decisions. When it came to buying the house, it was a given that she was very, very involved and helped us immensely and I can't thank her enough for that.

Love it. Do you have any investments?

I have about $42,500 in super which my auntie looks over to make sure it's invested to get the best return on shares. I took out $10,000 during COVID, but knowing what I know now, I wish I hadn't.

I had about $6000 of debt and I paid that off and then I put the rest towards our house savings account. So it helped with that; I didn't use it to go and spend on silly things. At this point I've only put about $5000 back in. I want to work on being more consistent at putting a little bit in each week or each fortnight.

Do you have any other debts?

My fiancé and I have a mortgage which is about $430,000. We only bought the place six months ago and the interest-rate rises have not been fun! Luckily though, my auntie stays all over it. My fiancé's parents offered to go guarantor to help us out, which was really amazing. We probably wouldn't be in the position we are without them as we wouldn't have had enough for a deposit. So we were very lucky there and that allowed us to have a little bit of a smaller deposit so we could spend money on furniture and setting ourselves up. We also bought a brand-new, top-of-the-line Isuzu D-Max and we owe about $60,000 on that. However, we actually put it up for sale last night.

Really? Why did you do that?

My partner changed jobs recently and we took quite a significant pay cut for long-term gain. Once he gets off probation, he's going to be earning commissions which will ultimately put us in a better place. We sat down and worked out what expenses we could minimise and what our goals are and realised that having an expensive car at the moment just doesn't really align with our goals. We should have thought about that six months ago before we bought it, but we didn't think that far ahead. We got so caught up in the moment of getting our first-ever, brand-new car off the showroom floor that we didn't forecast what would happen. So we made the decision this week to sell the car. It was hard, but it's the best thing for us at this point in time.

She's *on the* Money

A lot of people in the same situation, especially where the car's only six months old, would be so emotionally invested in the vehicle and other people's opinions that they'd be like, no, we can't get rid of it. It's too new, it's too this, it's too that.

It takes a lot of guts to step back and adjust your plan, to make new financial decisions that take the holistic and long-term view into consideration. Too often we get too caught up in our egos and start worrying, Oh what might people think if they see us buying a car and then selling it within six months?

Being able to own your mistakes and to make moves to correct them is so mature. Very wise and very brave.

When I told a few of my friends this week who knew how excited we'd been when we got the car, to be honest, I was a little bit embarrassed. But then when I step back and look at the bigger picture, I'm not embarrassed because we are putting us first. We're making the best financial decision for us and our goals and having that expensive car isn't doing anything to contribute to those goals right now. So what's the point of spending the amount we're spending each week to run this car when our goals are a wedding and building an emergency fund and starting a family in the next few years?

That makes me so happy. It sounds like you have some really good money habits, so what do you think your best money habit is?

I'm very frugal. I shop a lot when things are on sale and I shop around. If I need pet food, say, I'll look around at where it might be on sale. I try not to pay the highest price for things and I budget that way. I also do some online surveys every now and then to earn money towards fuel or groceries. I think that's my best money habit. I'm also frugal when we get bills – I'll look over them and if something doesn't look right, I'll question it. I always like to know where my money's going and that it's working for me in the best way possible.

It sounds like you're super resourceful rather than super frugal. But tell us about your worst money habit.

When it comes to other people I just spend; you know, on birthdays, Christmas and presents. I don't ever really question myself when it comes to spending money on others, I'll just transfer the money out of my savings account. I probably need to get a little bit better when I put money in there. I call it my little buffer but then I'll just transfer out. So I'm a giver. I'll spend money on other people without question, but I will always question it if I'm going to buy something for myself.

Now there's a mindset I'd like to see you work on. We care about everybody else, which is really sweet, but we need to care more about ourselves sometimes too!

At the start you said your money grade was a B minus. But we've heard that you're an accounts clerk working overtime and doing Uber Eats and online surveys to bring in more income. You have $42,000 in superannuation, a mortgage you're on top of and you're selling a car because, screw my ego, my financial future's more important. Do you really think you're a B minus?

Maybe not. Maybe an A minus.

The Pressure to Be Perfect

This money diarist recently quit a toxic but well-paying tech job to run a small property business with her dad. She's just 24 years old, has already bought her first home and, although you might think it sounds all peaches and cream, as a first-generation immigrant she still struggles with comparing herself to her peers who've followed more traditional career paths. Has she made the right call?

The first question I always ask is what grade you'd give your money habits?

I think I'd give myself a B. I'm good, but could be better.

Can you tell us a little bit more about your money story?

I'm a first-generation immigrant and grew up without much money at all. I moved here from China with my mum and dad when I was five. I couldn't speak English and, without the help of some really nice ESL teachers, I would've been way out of my depth. But it's probably easier coming to a new country as a young child because you're like a sponge and just soak everything up. Within a couple of years, I was like any other kid in the playground, but those first years were really tough, especially for my parents. They were both uni educated, but when they came here they basically had to start from scratch. They were working in factories and doing delivery driver jobs and trying to earn an income to support the three of us.

When we first moved here we were living in a tiny flat, sleeping on a mattress on the floor. It was bare bones at that time, but being a small kid you don't really notice that sort of thing – being with your mum and dad is all that matters. I also remember, despite being in a not-so-great area of town, we had really lovely neighbours. Most of them were immigrants as well and they would leave me second-hand toys and books outside our front door. So my first impression was that this place is great: people just give me free stuff! I think they felt sorry for us. Despite not having much themselves, they were all still willing to band together as a community and make the newcomers' lives a bit easier, which I find really heart-warming.

My parents worked really hard and their hard work paid off because they started a wholesale imports business and bit by bit it started to grow, until eventually it was able to sustain our family. But it wasn't until I was well into my late teens that my family's financial situation really improved. By then, my siblings were sent to private schools and we took family holidays every year. But growing up, I did not have any of those privileges.

I have one sister who is four years younger, my other sister's eight years younger, and my little brother's 12 years younger. Because of the way that my parents hustled – head down, making just enough money to survive and put food on the table – I grew up with the motto that money's meant to be saved, not spent. And if it is spent, then it should be on necessities only, which I guess is a solid mindset. But it affected me later on when I had my own money. I would get spending anxiety even about necessities like bills or groceries or food. I'd put off paying bills to the last day, for example, just to stretch the money out, even though I knew I'd eventually have to pay it.

She's *on the* Money

Spending anxiety is really common among people who haven't come from money. When they finally *do* get it, they find it really hard to part with and can feel especially guilty spending money on themselves. Such anxiety can become crippling and it certainly doesn't put you in the best possible financial position.

Rationally, if I sat you down when a bill arrived, you'd agree it would be best to pay it. You'd be like, absolutely, Victoria, get it off my plate! Yet, internally, you have this mental anguish playing against that. You're thinking, but if I pay it, the money's out of my account – and what if something happens and I need the money for something?

This is where setting up an emergency fund can be so useful. It creates a buffer, which not only gives you that feeling of security, but also helps you get on with managing the rest of your finances sensibly. No more late fees or interest penalties and, most importantly, it brings you peace of mind.

What do you do for work and what's your income?

I used to earn over $125,000 a year in a tech company, but today I run a small property management business with my dad. He's my sole business partner. We specialise in short-term and vacation rentals and we help our clients with everything, from setting up their property and marketing it, to managing the bookings, guests and housekeeping. Because it's just the two of us, we wear a lot of hats.

I currently pay myself $55,000 plus super, plus a 10 per cent profit share. Although that's what we have agreed on paper, I'm actually thinking of putting that 10 per cent back into the business, because at this point, investing in the business and helping it grow is my priority. With the way I live, even after taking a pay cut, I'm able to maintain my current lifestyle.

It would have been a big shift moving from a good income and job security. What made you change careers and how did you feel about going out on your own?

I definitely wasn't feeling confident about it at the start. Doubts came up, but after talking to mentors and other people who have run businesses, I realised that 'imposter syndrome' is quite common. To keep it manageable, I calculated the amount I would need to live on and cut down a lot of my expenses. I moved from my very nice apartment in the city into the suburbs where my partner lives. Sharing living costs has really helped with budgeting. I don't have a very glam life apart from taking a holiday every year – I'm not going out to fine dining or high-end places or shopping a lot. I'm lucky in that my lifestyle has always been quite manageable. The downside is, I'm not saving as much or investing as much, but I sort of think of it the other way around, which is that I'm investing in the business instead and it will deliver the biggest returns in the future.

Wow, how did you learn to structure a business in such a smart way? Most people just take cash out of the business to pay the bills, don't pay themselves super and are definitely not talking about profit share, especially this early on. Where's this come from? Why are you so smart?

It's a combination of my dad already having run a business in the past, albeit in a completely different industry. But he knew the process: setting up an ABN, setting up an ACN and all of that. He already had a business accountant, so we were able to tap into them too. Everything else came from researching, digging through Google, and also just from my past experiences – working in my day jobs since graduating. I've worked in marketing, I've worked in consulting, and most recently in tech. I observed the structure of those companies – some were large organisations, some were start-ups – and I was exposed to different areas in each business. The start-up, for example, had options for employees to buy shares and become part of the business and participate in their profit-share scheme. So I learnt a lot from experience, too.

Why property management?

When I left uni, dad bought an investment property that he wanted to live in after retirement and use occasionally as a holiday home. I helped him set up its online management and he asked me if I wanted to keep helping as a side hustle. The intention was for it to be 'set and forget' – just one property running itself without too much overhead, but I soon realised that there's a totally different level of risk running a short-stay rental versus a long-term lease. While a long-term lease is set and forget – you just want someone who pays the bills on time – with a short-stay rental there's communication with people coming in and out, organising housekeeping schedules, and marketing. In the high season you can attract more bookings, while in the low season you set different pricing strategies.

It was trial and error for the first few months, but we did well and were noticed by other property owners nearby who asked us if we'd manage their properties. So we started managing a few more. Once it started to grow, we realised our infrastructure was at breaking point. Our operating processes and procedures were bare bones, basically just an Excel spreadsheet with a bunch of random formulas that I made. I could have buffed up the tech more, but I was also juggling a full-time job, so I just didn't have the time or energy to do it. I was just bootstrapping for a while. Because my intention had always been to keep it as a humble side hustle, I didn't invest that much into it in the beginning.

The turning point was when the tech job I was in started getting toxic. The place was full of politics and a lot of red tape. It was a large organisation with a poor work culture and I was coming home mentally and emotionally drained every day. I knew it was bad, but at the same time I was getting paid a good salary! It took a lot of convincing from my partner, but finally I made the switch. I found it hard because, for a long time, I was still so focused on the money.

Earning $125,000 at age 23. I don't know if I could have walked away from that.

Yeah, exactly. But after being emotionally drained every day, I was wondering if it was actually worth it. I knew I didn't need a lot of money to just live my normal lifestyle. I was saving a lot, which was good, but at the end of the day, it wasn't the life that I wanted to lead. I finally realised that work-life balance and mental health were more important than reaching some really high, arbitrary income figure.

You learnt a lot about what you didn't like and what you wouldn't accept. Even though the experience didn't feel great, I'm sure it'll pay off in the future.

I look back and realise that I'd pinned a lot of my self-worth to my achievements and how much money I was making. It's really dangerous to think that way, especially if what you're doing no longer fulfils you. If you stay in a job you hate just for the money, your self-worth or your sense of self gets chipped away because it's so inextricably tied in your mind to your achievements.

I'm so excited that you made the change. Can you tell us a bit more about your big money goals?

My big money goal right now is purchasing our next home with my partner within four to five years. We already each own a property, but I'm hoping that by then we'll both have enough borrowing power and have saved enough to make that bigger purchase. We might have to sell one or both properties. Depends how we go.

Can you tell us about your investments?

I have one investment property that I bought about a year ago at a very low interest rate. I get about $20,000 in rental income every year. I'm really not looking forward to when the fixed-rate period runs out and I have to face reality!

How much did you have to save to purchase it and how did you decide that it was the right investment for you?

To be honest, I wasn't actively saving for this first home. I was living with my parents, which I'm super lucky to have done, and wasn't paying rent or bills, so I managed to save a 20 per cent deposit. The apartment was $570,000, so the deposit was just over

$100,000. I was working part-time while I was at uni, so couldn't save all that much then, but then I went full-time and was still living at home for over two years. It was during the lockdown, so that was a massive help.

Even if I'd wanted to, there wasn't much I could have blown my money on. I know a lot of people suffered during lockdown, but I don't think I would've been able to save for a deposit otherwise. I wasn't really thinking about buying a property, but I'd saved all this money and the interest rates were really low. It was a big incentive to jump into the property market and I was encouraged by family who were saying that I had the cash and interest rates were low, so why not do it. I know there's risks to that as well, because they won't stay low forever, but it was a big motivator at the time.

So often, people are saving even though they don't know what for and then all of a sudden things fall into place. That's why we need consistent savings goals.

Do you have any other investments, if so, what are they and how did you get into them?

I invest in stocks – ETFs and shares – which I also started doing during lockdown. I've got about $22,000 in ETFs and shares. It's gone up a bit from the time I put it in, which was during the crash, so I've been lucky. I just researched articles online and asked friends and family what they were investing in.

And tell us about debts. Do you have any? If so, what are they?

I've got the mortgage on my property – I really should calculate how much my repayments will go up by and what impact that will have on my lifestyle. I've just been putting it off because the thought seems very scary. I also have my HECS debt, although I'm not loving the indexation on that right now. Currently it's sitting at just over $8000.

What are your best money habits?

I think it's the combination of having a high interest bank account and a credit card. I use the credit as a financial tool and don't consider it as debt because I've never been late on a payment, plus I see the points I earn as free money. I have most of my money in a high interest bank account so I get the interest, but then I also get the credit card points. Right before my credit card bill is due, I pay it off in full so I don't get any fees. Because I accumulate a fair amount of points, I also get bonuses when I sign up for other cards. I've cashed out $400 or $500 worth of vouchers so far.

Money win, that's free money and a smart way to use a credit card. But we need to know, do you have any bad money habits?

Unfortunately, I do. My worst money habit is not really having a solid plan for investing. I get the basic concepts of putting money into shares, but I keep forgetting to do it regularly and don't have a solid strategy for doing it. So, for example, every time I've invested in shares, it's literally because I'll be having a conversation with family, or a friend, or my partner and suddenly remember, oh yeah, I have shares and should probably check in on them. It's been a while. And then I log on, and I might make one or two trades, and then I just forget about it for the next six months. I'm lucky in that, overall, I haven't made a loss, but there have definitely been certain stocks that haven't performed as well.

Do you still think your money grade is a B? And what would it take to get you to an A?

I think I'll upgrade it to a B plus because you've fluffed me up a little bit! To get to an A, I need a more solid plan for investing. I think my exposure to investing when I was younger was to focus on real estate, which is what our parents taught us, but it's not as feasible for me to just build a real estate empire. Other forms of investments, like shares, are a lot more accessible, so I feel like if I actually did more research into the share market and was more diligent with it I could get myself to an A.

She's an Egg Donor and an Inspiration

This money diarist is a 36-year-old New Zealand mother of two and the first on the Māori side of her family to graduate from university. Not only that, she's also an emergency services worker *and* an egg donor. What a rockstar!

First question, please tell us a little bit about your money story?

I'm one of five kids and we grew up in a very small rural town of less than a thousand people in the South Island of New Zealand. Dad worked very hard, but money was extremely stressful growing up; there was always arguments about it. Looking at all that stress, I knew that in order to live the life I wanted, I needed to get a good career. As a child, I'd say I was very stressed and pessimistic about money, but over the past five or so years, I've become more optimistic.

So you're changing your narrative, from past you to future you?

Absolutely. Yep.

What do you do for work and how much do you earn?

I'm a part-time paramedic and I'm on about $106,000. I'm paid on a pro-rata basis because I'm part-time. And that's not including super.

Paramedics don't get enough credit; you guys do such a special job. Do you love what you do?

It's challenging and every day is different. I'm coming up to 12 years in the job and obviously the COVID pandemic was stressful for everyone. As such, I had a period where I struggled with the workload, particularly when I had a few family members who died.

I was burnt out, so I saw a psychologist, who I still see, and she's fantastic. She told me I needed to take some time off: either go on WorkCover or use my sick leave, so I took about eight weeks off work. She didn't want me to get to the point where I'd end up totally exhausted, off work and couldn't get back on the road. She knows paramedics who've had two years off and still can't get back on the road because they completely burnt out. I'm in a much better place now. I'm back at work and feeling much better.

I'm glad you reached out and got help. We need to identify burnout earlier and give ourselves the self-care and the space to get through it.

You're absolutely right. And we need to normalise it by talking about it. I talk very openly to my colleagues because all of us need help at some stage. And I talk to my family about it, whereas growing up, mental health was just never talked about. Everything was swept under the rug.

What's your big money goal?

My husband and I are very fortunate in that we already own a house. He's also a paramedic and we've both got some long service leave coming up. Our big money goal is that in 2025 we're planning to take a year off and live overseas with our two kids. We'll be able to do half pay for some of it and then we'll use some annual leave.

Oh my gosh, that's so exciting. Where are you going?

We're very disorganised, but we plan to base ourselves in Italy. We're so privileged. I can't even comprehend how lucky we are. We both know this, how very fortunate we and our kids are. We're very lucky.

Hmm, I don't think luck comes into it. You have this plan you're working really hard towards and you'll have earnt it. Do you have any investments?

Absolutely, we have super. The last time I checked it was about $150,000. In the last couple of years I've also started investing in shares. I made sure I did a lot of reading up before I dipped my toe in. At the moment I think my shares are around $35,000.

Very nice. How did you get into the market? What made you take that step and how did you pick your assets?

I love to read and I believe that knowledge is power. So I just read a lot of financial books and listened to podcasts including

She's on the Money of course! Ultimately, you've got to figure out what works best for you. I didn't want to overwhelm myself with which platform was the right one, so I ended up going with CommSec, even though some of their fees were a bit higher compared to others. I then researched blue chip stocks and ETFs that felt solid.

The majority are in the S&P 500, a decision influenced by Warren Buffett's advice. I'm not about picking random stocks or following someone's 'hot tip' on what stock is going to be the best. I just did my own research and thought, you know what – I'll do $1000 lots in my first year, and then probably an ETF of some kind or a listed investment company that I believe to be good standard stocks, and then I'll reinvest the dividends.

Queen! I love that. Do you have any debts?

Obviously the mortgage, which is about $400,000 at the moment, but no consumer debt. We got rid of that quite a few years ago, paid off our cars and all of that. I have a student loan from New Zealand which I should have paid off years ago. I've actually made a goal for myself to pay it off by June next year and already have $16,000 set aside. I think the loan is $31,000 which I'll just knock out of the park.

I love that you've got a plan for it. What's your best money habit do you think?

When I set goals, I get that tunnel vision and just do it. So, for example, I've set this goal of paying out my student loan and I know I'll do it by June.

Great! Now tell us about your worst money habit?

I take money out of savings sometimes, generally to spend on food like takeaways. That's probably the worst one at the moment.

That's not too bad. What grade would you give your money habits?

I think it would be a solid B. We're on the way to being very financially stable.

What would you have to do to get to an A?

I'd have to have the student loan knocked out and maybe the mortgage reduced a bit. We've already got our emergency fund so I feel that that's not a problem, but it's just those other things.

I want to know about your emergency fund. Have you always had one? If not, why?

I find this fascinating. Everyone's emergency fund will be different. From what I've read, it's anywhere from three to six months' of living expenses. I set ours at a minimum of $25,000.

We put about $200 a fortnight into that and plan to let that keep ticking away. I originally set a goal of $25,000, but then you think maybe it should be higher. But I guess if there's always a minimum of $25,000, I'll be happy. Any excess, I'll just put into shares.

She's *on the* Money

Continuing to contribute to and build up an emergency fund once you've reached your target amount is an ambitious approach. At the opposite end of the spectrum, other people I speak to tell me they don't think they need an emergency fund at all, because they have a credit card – which kinda misses the point.

The idea of the emergency fund is somewhere between salary and insurance. It's a buffer that gives you peace of mind, knowing you have up to 6 months of income set aside in case you can't work, before insurance kicks in, and/or to cover any unexpected expenses.

For me, personally, the idea of relying on credit cards for that kind of thing gives me mad anxiety – it's a short-term loan, potentially on very high interest, which you have to pay back. But different things work for different people and as much as I genuinely believe that every single human needs an emergency fund and would love, love, love it if we all had one, the critical thing is to be educated on all your options so you make the best choice for you.

So long as you've factored in the ability to cover your expenses for three to six months without your income, then that's what you're aiming for.

You said that growing up your parents argued a lot about money. What did you take from that? Was it overwhelming? And how does that now affect the conversations you have with your partner about money?

There was definitely a lot of anxiety about money growing up – mainly around the unknowns, like, could we continue to afford renting where we were? But there was always food and we always had a roof over our heads. Typical of a small town community, there was always support and we had a lot of family, so we were privileged in that respect. But for a long time into my twenties I held onto that anxiety. When I was working, I wasn't fantastic with money because we weren't taught about it. I spent all that I earnt and didn't think about my future self in terms of putting money aside. My sister and I always knew that we needed to get good jobs as a way of ending the cycle of being financially unstable, so that was my first step. But even with a good career and earning decent money, that doesn't mean that you know what to do with it or that you're going to be financially stable and independent.

So true. Do you still feel anxious when people talk about money?

A little bit. Over the years it's reduced. Once we paid off our car loans and credit card debts, the anxiety started to go away. It's amazing the weight that lifts off your shoulders by doing those things. A lot of that anxiety has gone for sure because we don't have that consumer debt anymore. We now have a really decent emergency fund, we have good super and we have a goal as to what we're doing in terms of investing for our future. So I don't have the anxiety now.

I know that you're an emergency services worker and an egg donor. Can you tell us more about that?

It's a long story, so I'll try to condense it. When my husband and I decided to try for a family, we were very realistic, probably because of the jobs we do. So we talked about what would happen if we couldn't conceive naturally. This was back in 2013. We talked about IVF, we talked about other fertility treatments, egg donations from another woman, adoption, all of it. It got me thinking about my brother who's gay and lives in London with his partner. I said to my husband that if my brother ever wanted to have a family one day, I hoped someone would donate the eggs. Having children is incredible and I started thinking perhaps I could do that for someone else, knowing that someone might do that for my brother and his partner if they wanted kids too, in future.

Fast forward to 2017 and my husband reads an online article about a couple of Aussie guys – 'the boys' I call them – who were looking for a Māori egg donor and weren't getting anywhere because it's obviously very niche. My husband asked me what I thought about it. At that time I was 31 and, I know I'm not old, but obviously your number of eggs and their quality starts reducing with age, especially after 35. We decided to email them and throw my hat in the ring. I explained who I was and about my family, what I do, what tribe I descended from in New Zealand and a whole lot of other information.

Turns out they had an overwhelming response from women in New Zealand and in Australia of Māori descent – I think over 70 women responded. Not all the women met the criteria in terms of age and so on, but my email was lucky last, which I think caught their eye. It was a bit of a process for them, but in the end, they narrowed it down to five women. From there we had to go to our GPs and get lots of blood tests done, looking at how many eggs we had left and so forth. A couple of women didn't quite meet the criteria and, in the end, it came down to a personal decision for them and they picked me. Unlike in America, in Australia egg donations and surrogacy sperm donations are not commercial, meaning you don't get paid for it.

So it's altruistic; you do it because you're a kind human?

Absolutely. But the boys paid everything associated with the process – the IVF medications, the GP visits, the blood tests, the ultrasounds, all the flights to Queensland for the egg retrieval et cetera, the accommodation, the food, everything. Any days I had to take off work were all covered too. I mean, they treated me like an absolute queen! And we have a fantastic relationship. I've actually done IVF twice for them and now they have a little girl.

She is just over two now. I've met her and you just don't know how you're going to feel because she's come from me. But it was beautiful. It was emotional, obviously, but I didn't feel like I needed to take her home and that she was mine. It was just . . . yeah, she's just a very special little girl.

Is this something that you'll continue to do?

That's a really good question. For me, personally, it was always going to come down to having a connection with the couple. I always wanted to donate to only one couple, whereas I know other women who've donated to multiple couples. In Victoria, the law is you can only donate to a maximum of 10 families including your own.

And are your brother and his partner going to have a baby at any point?

I hope so. They both adore their nieces and nephews. First, I want him and his partner to get married. I want to go to a wedding, I want to have a party!

First Nations, Remote Community to Now a CPA!

This money diarist is a 33-year-old First Nations woman who grew up in a remote Indigenous community and was surrounded by the cycle of welfare dependency, drug and alcohol abuse and domestic violence. With dreams of creating a different life for herself, she moved to the mainland and pursued a financial education. She's now a certified practising accountant (CPA) and proud home owner.

What grade would you give your money habits?

I think I would be a B or a B minus.

Okay. Can you tell us a little bit more about your money story?

My money story starts with where I was raised. I'm an Aboriginal woman from an island off the east coast of Brisbane in Queensland. I come from a small Indigenous community that is really quite welfare dependent. Drug and alcohol abuse and domestic violence are pretty rife too. I grew up knowing that I didn't want that, which is hard, right? Because you grow up with families and you grow up with friends who are part of that and will always live there. But as soon as I could, I knew I wanted to escape and get out of the community to create a different life for myself.

On the other hand, I knew I would always come full circle and that depending on what I did and how I went about it, I would bring something back to my family, my sister, her children and my children when I have them. Being Aboriginal, you talk about intergenerational wealth and the fact that it's not there, especially in communities that are so heavily welfare dependent, and so, regardless of what I earnt, I always wanted to be able to return and give back to the people who helped me.

Did you have any role models in your family – how did you know that you wanted to create a different life for yourself?

It definitely comes back to my parents. My dad has his own business. And you know how one of your She's on the Money principles is about saving pennies – from little things, big things grow? . . . Well, he was always really focused on how much everything cost, right down to the last cent, which, as a child, always annoyed me. Whenever we went to Woolies or Coles it'd take forever – he'd be price checking everything. So he was an influence, but I think the biggest role model for me was my mum. From a very young age I could see the sacrifices she made for us so we could do the things that we wanted to. She and my dad sacrificed a lot to support us, not just when I was at school, but when I was at university as well. The things they helped me do and the money my mum snuck me without my dad knowing helped so much.

Do you know much about your dad's childhood?

My Aboriginal background is on my mum's side and my dad's side is white. His family were actually Swedish and he grew up in Horsham in Victoria. They were very poor. His meal was basically going out into the country and shooting rabbits; that was often the only way that they could eat. He's quite private about his life growing up. I know that in his teenage years his parents divorced. So that would've brought more strain, going from a dual income to a single income when they were already struggling.

How about your parents?

They met when they were 16 and married when they were 18, so they basically grew up together. My mum came from a welfare-dependent family. Her dad passed away when she was 16 and he'd been the income earner. She was one of seven kids and they quickly fell back into the welfare cycle. I've seen the house she grew up in – it was a tiny two-bedroom shack – and I can't imagine how you could fit all those kids in there.

I know in communities we talk about social housing and overcrowding being an issue, but there are pros and cons. You're very connected with your family in a situation like that and that's great, but of course there are inequities that come with social housing as well.

My mum's mum was part of the Stolen Generations and so I think for her it was all about trying to move forward and create a better life for her children. Her dad had been blackbirded from Vanuatu, which has since been recognised by the Queensland government as wage theft. So the couple of generations before me were really conscious about building wealth for their families.

Do you think that history impacts you today?

One hundred per cent. There's no generalised way that you can articulate how you're different to white Australian or Asian communities, or other cultures either – my husband is Tongan and that differs from other Polynesian communities. You just grow up knowing that this is how you do things, that it's all about that connection, whether it be a connection to culture, a connection to family, or a connection to community. Basically, what's yours is mine. The only way I got ahead was because of my family. So if I can show them thanks in some way, then why wouldn't I do that?

That is so beautiful. So tell us a bit more about you. What do you do for work and how much money do you earn?

I'm a CPA – a certified practising accountant – and a senior manager at PwC Indigenous Consulting. We're a separate legal entity to PwC – they own 49 per cent and we own 51 per cent. So we are self-determining, but obviously affiliated.

I'm on a salary of $180,000. So very, very blessed.

Just out of uni, I started off at a smaller Indigenous organisation. It was a peak body at the time. That's when I started studying to be a CPA. I worked there for a couple of years, then moved across to where I am now, and I've been here for eight years. I moved up the ranks, from the associate grade up to senior manager. There are now only two positions above me – director and partner – so there's still the ability to take on more responsibility and increase my salary.

You have to work really hard at one of the 'big four' consultancy firms. It's competitive and there are so many people that are incredibly hardworking and really high performing. In order to show your worth and prove your value, you do have to work above and beyond. In an Indigenous business where around 60 per cent of us are Indigenous, really being able to step up and show your value takes hard work.

Do many people in your family have degrees?

I'm one of very few people from our community to go to uni and get a degree. At the time I went, 10 or so years ago, there would've been maybe one in every three of us that went. So it's something I don't take lightly at all, and I'm incredibly grateful for it.

Around the time I enrolled, my family bought a little $300,000 house on the mainland that we could use when we were at university. All we had to do was fill the fridge, basically, to look after ourselves. So I didn't have to stress about rent and all those extras. My mum and dad just wanted me to focus on my studies. I was very lucky that I was able to do that.

My husband and I were eventually able to buy that house off my parents. We met in 2015 and pretty much moved in together straightaway. My parents offered to sell us the house for $100,000 less than the market value.

That's so generous of them.

It really was. So we took the opportunity, knowing we'd have to renovate it in the future, and leveraged it to buy an investment property. At the time, my salary was around $50,000. I often think about that and how my salary, as just one indicator, has increased so much since we bought that house eight years ago. So I'm pretty blessed and lucky and very proud of what we've done because that's meant we've able to take another step towards building that intergenerational wealth.

Do you ever look at it and go, it's not luck, it's actually bloody hard work?

That's a really interesting point because I think there are a lot of stereotypes about Aboriginal people owning homes and how apparently we get all sorts of help, like a really good interest rate or what have you. When I went through the process of buying this house, the only advantage I received was that I'm a CPA accountant which positively affected my LMI. The fact that I'm Indigenous played no part in it.

In our case, you have to reel it back to understand how hard we've worked. I've been on a salary all my adult life, but there was a time in our relationship where the amount of hours my partner worked to put us ahead so we could really start paying off some of the loan, leverage the equity and add more money to our renovation fund was huge. We lost so many weekends together.

So yeah, you're right; it's not all luck, it's about being able to sit back and acknowledge just how hard you've worked.

I wholeheartedly agree. Now, let's pivot. What are your current big money goals and what are you working towards?

In terms of big money goals, the house that we're renovating is all well and good, but it will ultimately be rented out. We want to take advantage of that because we want to focus on our forever home. We got married recently and we want to be able to settle down and think about having a family, maybe not seven kids like my mum, just two or three!

My longer-term goal is, I want to be able to help my family. I have a little nephew, I have a little niece. My sister, if I can be honest, is caught in the welfare cycle and she's a single parent. I want to be able to focus on something like investing in bonds for them.

That's so good. Do you have any investments right now? If so, what are they?

Since we bought our home under market value, we could immediately leverage the equity to buy our investment property. Even though I'm an accountant and am pretty aware about this stuff, I'm starting to get a bit nervous that it's about to turn into a positively geared property. So we have to sit down and think about it soon.

She's *on the* Money

The equity in a property refers to how much of it you own versus what the bank owns, valued in today's market. For example, if your home is valued at $400,000 and you still owe $300,000, your equity is $100,000. Banks may let you use a portion of this as security against another loan, which is what our diarist did here, to purchase an investment property.

The financial planning around an investment property involves looking at the ways in which it will pay for itself. As well as rental income, this could include keeping the property negatively geared, which essentially means that the costs of holding the property – such as interest repayments, maintenance costs, strata fees and the like – exceed the income it generates. Investors use this difference to help reduce their taxable income.

And how about debts?

We're really lucky at the moment to have just two main lines of debt: the mortgage on our main property and the mortgage for the investment property. Both are under $300,000, so things are looking pretty good. We've just managed to refinance about $100,000 from our owner-occupied home to focus on the renovations. Other than that, I have no other personal debts.

What's your best money habit, do you think?

I don't know if this is an accountant thing, but I'm not very creative! So when my husband and I sit down and talk about what we want to do in terms of the renovations, for example, because I'm not a creative brain, I just can't think on the spot. So I'll quite often sit on purchases before I buy something. I think that's a good thing because it means you can really try to understand whether you need something or whether it's just an impulse buy because you've been told that you need it by Black Friday sales or the Instagram algorithm.

What about super and other investments?

I salary sacrifice into superannuation. If I remember correctly, my super balance at the moment is about $180,000. I salary sacrifice an extra $700 per month. Overall, that puts me just under the concessional contribution cap. I decided I wanted to reach the cap every year to see how much it can reduce my tax. Because I'm on $180,000, the more that we can do to reduce tax, the better and it doesn't make a huge change to my disposable income. The $700 is a buffer that I can pull out if and when we need to.

She's *on the* Money

Since She's on the Money is all about building financial freedom for future you, we love to talk about superannuation. If you're employed, your employer must pay at least 11 per cent of your 'ordinary time earnings' into your super account unless exceptions apply. But if, like many in our community, you're self-employed, it's even more important to take ownership of this for yourself.

If you can afford it, making extra contributions to your super can boost your retirement savings and reduce your tax. Even small amounts add up over time and voluntary contributions can reduce the amount of tax you pay. If you're on a low income, you may be eligible for extra contributions from the government.

You can choose to make personal contributions to your super in one of two ways: concessional, which is paid using pre-tax dollars, or non-concessional, which uses after-tax income.

Concessional contributions are taxed at 15 per cent (up to $27,000 per financial year or higher if unused limits from previous years apply). For those earning over $45,000 a year, this could mean paying less tax while boosting your retirement savings.

Non-concessional contributions are paid using your after-tax income. They can reach up to $110,000 in each financial year and may also qualify for a tax deduction. If you're a low to middle-income earner and make after-tax super contributions, you may be eligible for a matching contribution from the government, called a co-contribution. The government will work out how much you are entitled to when you lodge your tax return. If you're eligible, the government will pay the co-contribution directly to your fund.

And what about your worst money habit?

I would say good old UberEats. Which is really depressing because I think the food in our area isn't even that good! I'm terrible at meal prepping and I'm terrible at grocery shopping and absolutely hate it. It's probably childhood trauma from my dad checking every single price on every single item!

After everything you've told us, do you still think your money grade is a B or B minus?

When I think about how I've grown up, how I've gone to university and created a career for myself, that I have around five times the average super balance for Indigenous Australians my age, and that my partner and I will only continue to grow, I can be really grateful for how hard I've worked and what I've done. I'm also really grateful for my parents and the things they've provided along the way to help me achieve everything I have. So I would probably increase my grade to an A.

But, like I said in the beginning, there's always going to be different seasons of life where there'll be different financial priorities. I'd like to learn more about shares to be able to invest for my nephew and niece. And the whole conversation around childcare, if we have children, is another thing. If you put your kids in childcare, that's going to be a huge chunk of your salary and we'll need to plan for that. So different priorities, different things, mean that I always need to learn more.

Hope After Homelessness

Content warning: this story concerns mental health and addiction.

This money diarist was homeless at 17, then diagnosed with borderline personality disorder (BPD), post-traumatic stress disorder (PTSD) and irritable bowel syndrome (IBS). Fast forward several years and she's now stable and receiving NDIS support, is about to start uni, and has been working on a budget with her occupational therapist. She even has some savings and a small emergency fund to boot!

First things first. If I asked you to grade your money habits, what would you give yourself?

I'd probably give myself a C. I feel like I'm pretty average, but I try my best.

Can you tell us a little bit about your money story?

I was raised by a single mum on a disability support pension, so I grew up with very little as my dad didn't contribute financially. We lived in housing commission and money was something we didn't really speak about. If we did, it was usually out of frustration on my mum's part; the stress that she was going through trying to manage and survive.

I have two siblings, so money was always very tight. I didn't have enough for a Myki card and couldn't ask Mum for money, so I'd just fare evade because it was better to do that and it was way less stress. Things continued that way as I got older. When I hit 17, I couldn't cope with family life anymore. I'd spoken to a couple of support workers and they encouraged me to move out and to try to find some independence and a safer environment. My home life was heavily affected by drugs and my mum was getting a lot worse with her own mental health. I managed to find some amazing connections through a couple of youth organisations. They were really good and got me into a refuge.

The refuge wasn't far from where I used to live. I spent maybe six weeks there before getting government housing. I moved in with another person at risk and, for a little while, things started to feel a bit better, but then, gradually, I started to feel really negative. My emotions were fluctuating and things were overwhelming. I was trying to juggle study with finding permanent accommodation and working through my feelings, all at the same time. I reached out to my GP and told her I needed someone to talk to.

She pointed me in the direction of a psychiatrist who diagnosed me with borderline personality disorder which often gets confused with bipolar disorder, as they're quite similar. I was also diagnosed with PTSD and then with IBS and unfortunately had to quit studying for my diploma as it all became a bit too much. I got to a really low weight, about 39 kilos. So my GP said I had to stop my studies and just focus entirely on my recovery or I was going to end up in hospital. So I did, and then applied for NDIS funding for support.

I'm so glad you did that. Did you find securing NDIS funding a challenging process?

Yes, it took about a year and that was with someone helping me write the reports and advising my therapists what to put in their reports and what language to use, because they are very particular. I was knocked back once because my condition had only been diagnosed when I was 17, so they didn't believe that it was permanent. But in the end, once we provided more evidence, everything was okay.

What did you do in that 12 months before you received the NDIS support?

I used everything that I could. I don't really have much family support, other than my little brother. He's been a big part of my journey and is someone I can always rely on. I also relied on my GP, who's absolutely incredible, and on my psychologist, who I was able to see using the Medicare rebates. That made an absolute world of difference. Lifeline was great too. I want to say that you shouldn't feel any shame utilising those services, because that's what they're there for.

Apart from the NDIS support, are you working and how much are you earning?

I'm unemployed, but I do volunteer at a cat shelter. I have three cats at home and I'm a massive animal lover. Besides that, I do dog walking sometimes which my occupational therapist helped set up, and I'm hoping to continue that when I start my bachelor's degree, which I've just been accepted for. I'm going to study a bachelor of health science, majoring in disability and inclusion and psychology for allied health.

Congratulations! That's so exciting.

Yes, I'm over the moon. This is what I've been working towards and my focus is going to be entirely on that, while maintaining my support system. Hopefully I'll continue to grow and see where it takes me.

In terms of finances, what is your big money goal? What are you working towards?

My big money goal would be to go on a holiday! I've never been on a plane, so that's something I really want to do. Bali is my dream destination, so I've been working through some small goals with my therapist to help me gain the confidence to stay away from home for a few days. I'll eventually build up to being comfortable with being away from my cats for a week or so.

Another of my big savings goals is just having money for myself and my cats so that if anything goes wrong I can provide for us. My cat had to have her tail partially amputated recently, which came completely out of nowhere. She wasn't in any pain, but the vet noticed it when she went for her teeth cleaning. I could pay for that and that was important.

My cat getting sick was one of those things that you don't expect and I hadn't properly planned for it financially, so I'm glad I was able to find a way to make it happen. For me, there's a mental health cost too, so there's no way I'm not going to have my cat. I got her when I was 17 and she's been my absolute little angel, my saving grace all throughout everything that's happened.

As a pet lover myself, I completely understand! Next question is, do you invest?

Not at the moment, unfortunately. I do have $140 in a bank account which I've labelled 'investment funds', so I've got plans. I've bought your investing book and have spoken to my support worker who said she's going to help me set up my super so I can make contributions myself.

Hearing you talk about 'from small things, big things grow' really motivated me. I thought, why can't I just put $20 a fortnight towards that and see it slowly grow? Even though I haven't been working and contributing, I'm still trying to do my part.

She's *on the* Money

A lot of people who are either self-employed or unemployed tend to put super on the backburner. While it makes sense to feel that investing into a long-way-off future may not be in your best current interests, in such circumstances it could be worth considering how saving even small amounts might benefit your mindset.

For example, using round-ups (where your bank rounds up your spend to the nearest dollar and pops the difference into a savings account), could mean that you hardly notice the contributions you're setting aside. Yet, by doing so, you're building wealth and security for future you. Even the tiniest amounts over a period of time can really add up.

When we talk about money mindsets, knowing that you're investing in your own future can help give you a deeper sense of security and self-reliance. There's something really powerful in that.

Do you currently have any debts?

I have a study debt from when I did my diploma and didn't complete it, but I did get one credit point towards my bachelor degree, so it was worth something.

What's your best money habit?

I'd have to say it would be my resourcefulness. Growing up, it was very common for my mum to access services like Vinnies and the Salvos to help with grocery costs and food bills, so we always had food on the table. I also accessed them when I was homeless and struggling for money. I would try my best to cover rent and have enough money for my cats, then rely on them for additional support. I used all the resources that I had available to me and reached out when I needed to.

Now that I'm not having to use those services anymore, I'd say my best money habit is still resourcefulness, but it looks a little bit different. Rather than seeking support from those organisations, I'm now seeking support from my therapist and getting advice on how to budget better. I'm also getting support from you guys with regards to different finance tips and tricks.

Resourcefulness is incredibly powerful and one of the best money habits you can have. On the flip side, what's your worst money habit?

My guilty pleasure is that I love fresh fruit and vegetables – they're something I didn't have growing up. So now, when I go to the grocery store, I want the freshest and best fruit I can find. I don't want frozen veg, so I have to really make sure I'm sticking to my meal plan and budget. Otherwise I end up buying copious amounts of fruit and vegetables and then having too much food waste! That's probably my worst money habit.

Am I right in assuming that you're one of the first in your family to go to university and do a degree?

My auntie did a degree, but in my immediate circle, I'm the first one to do a bachelor's degree.

I feel like you're changing your entire narrative.

Yes, it's exciting. I've told my mum and my brother about the degree, but I'm yet to tell anyone else – I'm just keeping it on the down low. I'm still a bit shell-shocked by it to be honest. I'm not sure if it's really true!

You'll absolutely smash it. What do you think your grade would be now that we've gone through your money story? Do you really think you're a C?

I'd say I'm more a B because of how resourceful I am. I'm so excited to be able to study and then one day earn my own income and see how I grow. I feel like I'll be able to set myself up for a future that I never thought I would have. I only have so much to work with and I think I'm doing okay with what I have, and I'm extremely excited about my future.

We are too. My last question is what advice would you give to someone who's in a similar situation to you, when you were 17?

The biggest thing is just to reach out; to understand that you're not alone and that there are services out there that can help you. Just google what to do when you're homeless – that's exactly what I did – and resources will come up. There's a platform called Ask Izzy which is a government resource that you can access if you need food or shelter or assistance. It'll direct you to your nearest point of access. So don't stop and don't give up because you *are* worth it and it *will* get better. It just takes time and, unfortunately, a lot of waiting and a lot of pushing, but you have to advocate for yourself. It's definitely worth it.

MINDSET JOURNALLING PROMPTS

Define the difference between a 'scarcity mindset' and an 'abundance mindset'. How might you change your thinking to be more positive?

What money behaviours do you have that aren't serving you – like over-giving to others, or paying bills late, or under-spending on critical items. How will you change these?

What jobs or tasks make you happy? And which ones make you angry, sad or frustrated? Can you adjust your current work life to get more good and less bad?

Who and what resources can you can count on to support you financially and emotionally – from people, to learning tools, to organisations? Use them all the time, not just when times get tough but before then too, to keep you ahead of the game.

Mindset Money Wins

KIMBERLEA loves reading but felt like her collection was getting cluttered, so after a clear out she started doing weekly visits to her local library instead of buying books. She rediscovered the joy of browsing the library shelves, something she did every week with her dad when she was growing up. Love those nostalgic vibes.

While she was sick at home, **TRISH** used the spare time once she felt a bit better to sort out her finances. She took the time to learn how to set up her Sharesies account, and organised a salary sacrifice for her super. She also listed some bits and bobs on Facebook Marketplace and made back $70.

DAYNA spent a year educating herself on finance and looping her kids in for lessons too. They started doing chores to earn pocket money and decided to save up for a tablet. They soon achieved their goal and bought themselves the tablet!

EMILY bought one too many cocktails on a bougie weekend out (we've all been there!) and ended up with only $12 left in her bank account until she got paid later in the week. Before she became a fan of SOTM, she may have asked her family or boyfriend for money, but with her new money mindset she decided to get thrifty instead. Before a supermarket shop, she made sure she had used everything she could in her pantry. She went to Aldi, carefully calculated her purchases and managed to buy four items for $11.98 – bullseye!

SHANTEL learnt to plant, cook and preserve her vegetables! For her, it's a small continuous money win, as it helps her keep active (pulling weeds is a workout!) while also being crafty with what she grows and how she reuses the scraps.

AMY had her phone pick-pocketed while she was overseas and thought she would have to cough up for a replacement. She did some further research on her insurance policy included with her credit card and lodged a claim, not feeling too optimistic. Thankfully, she was reimbursed $1400 for her new phone, and was super glad she hadn't put submitting the claim in her 'too hard' basket!

HAYLEY heard on the SOTM podcast that if you email a hotel directly for a booking rather than going through a third party website you can usually get a better deal. She ended up not only with a reduced booking rate at a 5-star hotel, but free buffet breakfast for two, late checkout and an $80 voucher to use at the restaurant! You best believe she'll be doing this every time she travels from now on . . .

Inspired by a SOTM Facebook thread: Pay Off All Your Debt and Watch Your Confidence Soar, **HEATHER** was motivated to pay off her debt. Suddenly her situation felt exciting and rewarding. Now she is *loving* the soaring feeling!

CHARLOTTE put the power of banishing the shame around money into practice when her car unexpectedly broke down and she had to pay $3500 to fix it. She let her coaching service know what had happened and they were more than happy for her to be a touch late on her payments that month, which really helped take the pressure off.

SHANNON'S favourite money mindset lesson is reminding herself that she's not at the end of her story and that small changes now can have a positive impact on her future.

Lifestyle

Whether our lifestyle is one we're consciously creating or the result of an unexpected illness or event, outside factors have a huge impact on our financial security and stability. As a former financial planner, I'm obsessed with putting things in place to help smooth out any potential potholes along the road to financial success – from emergency funds, to insurance, to simply sitting down and mapping out your goals.

A sure-fire path to freedom is getting clear on your dreams and the steps you need to take to get there. This might mean breaking free from family patterns or self-destructive behaviours, or it could mean gaining an education or building self-worth to overcome seemingly insurmountable roadblocks. Once you start putting plans and protections in place and feel the thrill of small wins, the feeling is unstoppable.

Carrying the Pressure and Bridging Two Worlds

This 22-year-old first-generation immigrant from Sri Lanka is making a life for herself in Australia while juggling studying to be a psychologist at uni with paying the rent and all the associated costs of living. On top of that she's helping out her parents, one of whom is still in Sri Lanka, and neither of whom have any retirement savings. Caught between wanting to live a carefree student life and having to have her shit together to support her family, she's working *three* casual jobs while studying. No pressure!

First question, what would you rate your money habits?

I would probably give myself an A. I think I've developed some good money habits over my life. There are still some skills I need to work on, but I think I've done okay.

Can you tell us a little bit about your money story?

I have a bit of an anxious attachment to money, which manifests as a scarcity mindset. It's probably related to my childhood. Growing up, my family would have been classed as low income. My parents are really smart, skilled, hardworking people, but my dad isn't an Australian citizen and is still in Sri Lanka, so my mum raised my sister and me here in Australia on her own. My dad was the primary income earner and my mum had to stop working early because she had a workplace injury. Even then, before Sri Lanka's current financial crisis, converting his Sri Lankan income to Australian dollars wasn't great, so it was really hard for them.

Mum was predominantly a stay-at-home mum. Money was very tight growing up and there was a lot of rhetoric around affordability. I was very, very conscious of the concept of money from a young age. In saying that, I'm really grateful for where I came from and feel so blessed for everything my parents did for my sister and me. I genuinely don't feel like I missed out on anything as a child – the sacrifice was all on my parents' end. They didn't indulge in any discretionary spending, buying clothes or going out to eat, but they also didn't invest into their financial future in the conventional Australian way of super and investments. They funnelled all their money into my sister and me and our education. In a weird way, I feel like we're kind of their investments. So there's pressure to be a good return on that investment and be able to take care of them financially and help them retire and actually enjoy their lives.

Is there any plan in the future for your dad to join you guys here in Australia?

Eventually, yes, but in terms of what's going on in Sri Lanka right now and figuring out how to wrap things up in amongst that, he can't at the moment. We're waiting till my sister and I get full-time jobs and we start earning an income, so if he does leave, then we can cover things.

Can you tell us a bit more about what's going on in Sri Lanka and how it's impacted your family?

By May 2022 Sri Lanka was basically bankrupt – for the first time in its history, it failed to make an interest payment on its foreign debt. Because of resource shortages, people were struggling to access essential goods like food, fuel and medicines and experienced daily power cuts for 12 to 13 hours. Inflation was shocking, making food and housing affordability almost impossible. And the currency plummeted, worsening the financial situation of many families. As well as my dad, most of my family on my mum's side still lives there too. It's looking pretty grim in terms of how they're going to come back from that.

Has the situation in Sri Lanka shaped the choices you've made for yourself in terms of your career and the opportunities you're pursuing?

Definitely. I'm just trying to make sure that I finish my education as soon as possible and look for full-time work so I can help support my family. We have a collectivist culture in Sri Lanka where you don't really think about yourself but instead think about the whole family unit.

She's *on the* Money

On one hand it's important to recognise that buying into that cultural responsibility could feel like a lot to carry, but on the flipside, I never want people to feel like their parents or family are a burden.

Yes, it's a weight that you carry, but it's a choice as well. The aim is to lean into your values and culture and take both the blessings and challenges that they bring. Honouring your family and those commitments can also be a real strength.

This is why I always ask our community to check in with their value systems and know their money story: is your money story something you've inherited without thinking about it, or is it something you've taken the time to properly consider and chosen to adopt and consciously live by?

Likewise when it comes to judging yourself on your spending habits and choices. We all 'know' that there is usually a 'better thing' to spend our money on. Does that mean you shouldn't ever spend money on treating yourself? Absolutely not. Should you work through the decision and try to avoid impulse buys? Always.

It all goes back to becoming your best self, because when you are your best self you can fill other people's cups in the best possible way. If you feel really constricted, that's ultimately going to lead to some form of burnout or overwhelm in reaction to the responsibility that's on you.

It's about finding a happy balance and using our freedom of choice – consciously making decisions based our own personal values is the key to our success and happiness.

What do you do for work at the moment and how much money do you earn?

I'm studying full-time for a Master in Psychology, which takes up most of my time between clients and admin and classes. My main job is a tech position at my university and my second job is doing casual academic work. I teach a couple of tutorials after hours and also mark student assignments. My third job is doing some casual research assistant work for the lab that I did my honours with, which is really cool. My income varies depending on how many shifts I do, but it's between $500 to $1000 a week, so around $35,000 to $40,000 a year.

What is your big money goal? What are you currently working towards?

One of my short-term goals is to save a bit of money so I can maybe do some solo travelling after my master's because I didn't really do much of that when I was younger. My second goal is to buy an investment property one day. But honestly that seems so daunting! And I don't really have any financial mentors.

Do you currently invest?

I have around $15,000 in super. I've also got some stock investments as well. So, in total, I've got about $57,000 at the moment.

I was lucky in that I lived at home while I was an undergrad, so was able to save a lot on bills. But I'm proud of that. I've also got about $9000 in my emergency fund and that helps me sleep at night. Having that buffer is just so important to me. So I call it an investment.

Do you currently have any debts?

I don't have any personal debt or credit card debt, but I do have a HECS debt of about $34,000. It'll go up to $38,000 once I finish my master's. It's a bit stressful, but it could be worse: I know lots of psychology students who have HECS debts of $100,000 or more!

She's *on the* Money

HECS/HELP debt is a tricky one. As much as it's a debt that doesn't carry any interest, which is nice, it's still subject to indexation, so we do have to be careful of that. Especially with what we saw in 2023, when indexation reached 7 per cent – ouch!! Not to mention that carrying a HECS/HELP debt may affect the amount you can borrow for a home loan, too.

Still, I get why paying it off is not a priority for most people. I'm not making it a priority because it hasn't gotten in my way of creating wealth or buying a house, even though, thanks to several degrees, my HECS debt is more than $100,000. It does give me mad anxiety at times, but I also like the idea that if I wasn't making any income at all, the government wouldn't chase me for it, whereas that is definitely not the case with a mortgage or a personal loan.

That said, at the end of the day, it is still a debt, so it depends on how you view it and on your personal situation. I always say that some types of debt are better than others. A HECS/HELP debt that got you an education is arguably better than a credit card or buy now, pay later debt used to buy fast fashion. And an investment loan that bought you equity in an appreciating asset is what I consider 'good' debt, so long as you can afford to service it.

What do you think is your best money habit?

I'd say my best money habit is my work ethic and discipline when it comes to earning and saving money. I've been working since the age of 12 with netball umpiring and whatnot. I've always been a good saver, full credit to my parents, but I'm also very disciplined when it comes to spending money on things that I really value. So for example, I don't really value eating out all that much, so I'm really good at cooking at home and taking it into work. But on the other hand, I value living in a really nice space that's close to work and also I really value the gym! So I'll spend a bit more on those things, but then I'll save on other things that I don't really care too much about now.

Great. What do you think is your worst money habit?

Probably the guilt I feel spending money on discretionary things, knowing that there are people out there in far worse situations. It's stressful and you want to assimilate and do all these really fun things and go travelling and the like, but then you also think that money could be allocated to family who might need it more or used to build foundations for your future to give yourself some financial backing. I spent $100 on a night out the other week and I just was spiralling thinking about how much I'd blown!

But I know that's my inherited money mindset talking, so I try to remind myself that it's okay. I used to live in Victoria and I moved to Brisbane to challenge the idea that I always have to take the route that's going to be the cheapest and where I'm going to save the most money. I've taken actions that will force me to spend more money but allow me to grow in other ways. For example, on that night out, yes it wasn't all that productive, but I had a really good time and it set me up for a good week. I'm trying to reframe things, but it's definitely easier said than done.

So, what does the future look like for you?

I graduate at the end of next year once I've finished my master's.

I'm in the education and developmental stream at the moment and I'll be doing externships next year, so I think I'll get a better idea of what I'm actually looking into then. I don't think it'll be private practice – I feel it'll be more community-based work, giving back to others who need help.

I'm always looking out for ways to help my family and community, both here and in Sri Lanka, so that remains my number one priority.

I can't wait for you to find something that you love and adore and that will make you feel like you're having a really big impact. It is just another testament to how much of a special human you are.

A Humble and Huge Heart

Content warning: this conversation discusses things like eating disorders, domestic violence, abuse and depression.

This money diarist was raised by a single mum who experienced bankruptcy after leaving a domestic violence relationship with her dad, who's also a gambling addict. Overcoming her own mental health and health struggles, she's now working in child protection after nine years at university and is earning a full-time salary for the first time ever, aged 27.

What grade would you give your money habits if I asked you to give them a grade from A to F?

I think, probably, a C plus.

Can you tell us a little bit more about your money story?

I have two brothers. My dad was an alcoholic and also had a gambling addiction so we didn't grow up with a lot of money because he unfortunately spent most of his paycheque on his addictions. My mum did her best to keep the family running. When I was eight, she left him because of the domestic violence. For a while, things got a little worse financially. Having mum care for us on a single parent's wage was really difficult. And there was also a long court process, the divorce and splitting up the assets, which was messy.

At that age you only get to know a little bit about what's going on. Was it stressful as an eight year old to go through that?

It was very stressful. I think seeing your parents so stressed is hard. At the time, my dad was very keen on having my brothers, so there was a bit of emotional abuse too, where he'd read the court affidavits to us saying how bad our mum was, all that kind of stuff. Now, with some perspective, I can see that's not appropriate, but when you're young, you just accept it as Dad trying to share what was going on.

When I was 11 years old, my dad moved interstate and left us in my mum's care full-time, which came as a bit of a surprise. We didn't know it was coming. He just dropped us off one day, then all of a sudden we were living full-time with mum.

As a teenager, I developed some disordered eating mental health struggles. My mum has been so supportive the whole time, but it's definitely been a bit of a rollercoaster.

I got my first job at McDonald's when I was 15, working for $8 an hour. Because we'd struggled so much with money when I was younger, it felt like, hey, I've finally got some control here, I'm making my own money! It was a great feeling.

Then, when I was in high school, age 17, mum went bankrupt because she'd taken on a lot of debt to look after my brothers and me by herself, which had been really hard on her. During that time, she'd had another partner who'd unfortunately been abusive as well and very dependent on her. She left him, but was left with a lot of debt and so went bankrupt after that. So things got really rough for a while. But they're looking up now.

From the sounds of it, your mum backs you to the end of the earth but maybe doesn't look after herself in the same way that you get looked after. With her support around the disordered eating, are you okay if we talk a little more about that? As something I've experienced, I feel it's important to open up the conversation up around it.

Sure. I think I was conscious of my weight from very early on. It was actually something my dad criticised a lot. He was very fixated on my appearance, my mum's appearance and my brother's appearance, as he felt we were a reflection of him. So I think from early on I was quite self-conscious and wanted to change a lot about my body. The earliest age I remember feeling unhappy over something about my body was around four.

Wow, my heart. You shouldn't care about your body at four, you should be caring about sandcastles and chasing people and whether or not you can have ice cream after dinner.

Absolutely. And I can see all that now. But yes, I think that's probably where it first came from; wanting to be what *he* thought was 'enough'. My disorder started with lots of calorie restriction and over exercising. As my parents were going through their divorce and then with Dad moving interstate, this sense of trying to please everybody grew – I felt that my body was the only thing I could control. Especially before I got my job at Maccas, I didn't really have any other control other than doing really well at school. I think that controlling my weight was how I could prove that I was trying really hard. And I'm a bit of a perfectionist.

Did the job help you regain your sense of control and set you on your recovery journey?

Yes and no. I think for a while there I did feel like I had more control. As a teenager in high school I grew more of an identity as someone who did well at school, had a good group of friends, had a nice boyfriend at the time, and things were going well.

But in year 12, my disordered eating really hit its peak. I'd broken up with my boyfriend and I put a lot of pressure on myself to get the most perfect score so I could get into the best courses at uni. I wanted to study law originally, so the ATAR was quite high.

Looking back now, I realise I had no idea. I mean, it took nine years for me to get through uni! Now, I just laugh at myself. But at the time, I was putting a lot of pressure on myself to be perfect in every way I thought I needed to be. Trying to control my eating and my image was definitely a part of that.

Is it something you still struggle with today?

I've had a lot of therapy from age 22 until now, so a good five years. My relationship with food and with my body has improved a lot. When I was in the thick of my disordered eating, it was something I worried about constantly. Nowadays it might be a little thought that pops up every once in a while, but it doesn't control me. Back then, it was controlling me – the thoughts were controlling me. Now when they come up I'm like, no, we're not doing that. And I can push them aside.

She's *on the* Money

I've found therapy so helpful in managing my relationship with food as it wasn't something I could easily teach myself. Having someone come in and be like, okay, here are the strategies you need to implement, this is what we need to do to put you in the best possible position – that made a huge difference for me.

At the same time, I would hate for people to think that 'therapy cures you and you'll be completely over it.' We're a constant work in progress.

But once you have these strategies in your toolkit, when it pops up, you can go, no, no, no, we're going to quash that thought, this is not how we like to think, it's not what we are doing today.

From my own experience I'd like to suggest that if this is something you or a loved one is facing, reach out and get help as soon as you think you might need it. Places like the Butterfly Foundation are set up to help. It's worth it and so are you.

You said you're finally earning a full-time salary. What do you do for work? How much money do you earn?

I'm a social worker in a state-based child protection agency and I earn $72,091 a year. It's so much more than I ever dreamed of making when I was younger. I feel a bit strange about it to be honest.

Tell us about those nine years at uni. What degree did you do that led you to work in child protection?

I started off at uni when I was 17, just a little baby. My mum had to sign the permission slip so I could use the university computers, which is quite funny. I was taking on a lot of debt, so I think I was old enough to sign those forms myself!

I started off doing a double degree in international relations and arts and had dreams of being some kind of diplomat or maybe going into law, but I wasn't too sure. At the time I was also struggling with my mental health and had quite a lot of anxiety. Later I'd be diagnosed with an anxiety disorder and depression, but at that time I didn't know that, I just thought, why am I not coping?

I ended up dropping the international degree and going just for arts, but unfortunately failed quite a lot of subjects because I felt too anxious to go to class. I would try and go to the tutorial but then just walk straight past the door and go hide in the toilet stall because I was so anxious. This went on for quite a while before I reached out to my GP for help.

After that there was a bit of a learning curve, trying new antidepressant medications and new approaches to work out how to manage my anxiety so I could attend uni, but it was an uphill battle. For about three years I fluctuated between doing okay, then not doing okay. So I didn't end up finishing my arts degree until 2020. I wish I'd been a bit kinder to myself at the time and just done part-time uni and maybe gotten the help I needed a bit earlier. But we live and we learn.

Congrats though, how exciting, you did it!

Thanks, it was a long journey. At one point, I was quite interested in looking at portrayals of women's madness in literature and how that plays into society's views of women, but I studied social work instead. Witnessing my dad be very cruel to my mother fuelled that, I think. He often used to tell her she was mad or crazy. There wasn't really a lot of awareness of mental health from his part. It was just, you're crazy if you're struggling.

I had some time after I finished my degree to consider my next steps and realised I wanted to do something that could help. During COVID there were a lot of articles flying around about the increase in domestic violence and homelessness, but I think the pandemic just highlighted all the problems and systems that were failing already. I figured that I could help through doing social work. Then, after a year or two, I went into child protection because I thought it was an area I could make a difference in.

Oh my gosh, my whole heart. Knowing your background and where you've come from, that arguably you were a child that needed protecting, do you feel like this is your way of protecting kids that might be in similar circumstances?

I think so. I don't know if I'd have considered this work as an option if I hadn't done some reflecting on my own experiences as a child and noticed or recognised, with help, that there's been abuse there. I do want to help other kids. Obviously it's quite different in child protection, but knowing that maybe I could help protect them and ensure that they're safe and also work with families to make sure they have the right resources to keep their children safe as well – I feel like it will be really rewarding.

Tell us more about this role. What does your day-to-day job look like?

I've only been in it for about four months now and I've had two different roles in that time. The one I'm in at the moment is an assessment-based role. Notifications are screened in with concerns raised about the safety of a child. We'll go out and speak with the parents or whoever's involved, speak with the children and then possibly open an investigation from there. Once the investigation process starts it involves support partners. NGOs may become involved or, if at the end of the investigation it's deemed that the child is not safe where they are and their caregivers cannot provide safety for them, there may be a removal.

That's a lot to deal with on a day-to-day basis. How are you looking after you?

It's something that's evolved, my self-care routine. At first I had this whole list: I will come home and do meditation, or I will make sure that I'm doing yoga three times a week . . . and those things are all really good, but I think the best things I've done for myself are forming really great relationships with my colleagues and continuing to attend therapy.

When I get home sometimes I need to go onto the back lawn and just lie on it and look at the sky for a while to ground myself. I kick off my shoes and look up and feel like, it's okay, I'm still a person. I'm here. The world's bad, but not everything's bad.

Child protection is not something I entered into lightly and I'm actually quite new at the investigation and assessments role. I thought a lot about whether I could work in a system where Aboriginal and Torres Strait Islander children are still removed at a much higher rate than non-Indigenous children and with the history of the Stolen Generations, I just wasn't sure that was a system I wanted to be a part of. But my final year placement was with the department and it was through working there and seeing all the good work they do and working with Aboriginal and non-Aboriginal colleagues that I thought, okay, this is something I think I can do and feel okay about.

It's so important to work together, to rectify the past and change our futures.

Alright, let's move back onto money topics. What are your big money goals? What are you working towards?

At the moment, my biggest goal is just building up my emergency fund. It got so depleted while I was on placement as you have two full-time four-month placements where you're not earning any money, so I just want to build that up again. I'm also planning a trip to Japan and South Korea next year.

Can you tell us more about your emergency fund? How have you calculated how much you want in it – is it a month's worth of expenses, three months' worth of expenses? What makes you feel most comfortable?

For me, it's three months' worth of expenses and then I put $2000 on top of that because it just makes me feel better.

I really like that. Alright, next, do you invest?

I do invest, just a little. I have about $1000 in Spaceship which grew from when I was a student. I was only putting in about $5 a month as an investment in my financial education, but it's grown over time. The market has been quite brutal the last couple of years and seeing the market go up and down has given me the confidence of knowing it's okay, I can ride this; not to panic and withdraw my money at the wrong time. Then I have super as well.

That's the perfect example of why investing small amounts makes sense. Most of us working our very first job out of university don't have $1000 in an investment portfolio, but you do, and it's from all of those tiny amounts you saved during university.

Alright, talk to us about debt. Do you have any? If so, what is it?

I have a lot of HECS debt – I guess nine years at university will do that. So I have $74,315 in HECS and $10,172 in startup loans. Basically they're interest-free student loans. If you're getting any kind of Centrelink payment while you're at university, you can opt in for a startup loan of $1000 at the start of a semester which can go towards education costs.

What are you doing about that debt? Are you just letting it tick along or are you planning on making additional repayments?

At the moment, I'm just letting it tick along. I also found out – and this may help anyone who's struggling at uni and failing topics because of mental health or adverse circumstances at home – you can actually apply for a debt remission of some of your subjects if you meet the criteria. If you apply and it's approved, the debt will be removed for you.

That's a good money tip, which leads me to my next question. What is your best money habit?

I think I'm quite resourceful when I don't have a lot of money. I'm in a really good position now, but I haven't always been, so I'm quite happy to sell things online. When I was little, my brothers and I used to ride around on our bikes and collect cans because, in the state I live in, you can recycle them for money. Sometimes that would help us get dinner for the night, especially at Dad's house when there wasn't a lot of money.

Talk to us quickly about your money habits. Given you were so good at being resourceful and arguably very frugal, how have you found going from that lifestyle to having a $72,000 income?

I'm quite a bit better at budgeting than I used to be. We can all be good at money no matter what income, but it feels easier when you have a little bit more to play with. I have a lot less stress, which is probably the main thing. I'm very aware of lifestyle creep though. Previously I lived quite a restricted life because there wasn't a lot of money coming in, so now I want to make sure I give myself enough money to do some nice things, but at the same time, not spend it all. I found your Money Masterclass really helpful, so I have a very fancy spreadsheet now, which I'm very pleased with.

So good! I hate to bring down the mood . . . but what's your worst money habit, my friend?

Stress spending. Definitely guilty of that. In one of your early podcast episodes you talk about how, sometimes, when you haven't had a lot of money growing up, there can be that tendency to spend it when you have it. I've definitely felt myself default to that. If I'm not on top of my budget or if I'm not looking after my mental health and being aware of my self-care needs, I can just stress spend.

She's on the Money

We've been talking about it on the *She's on the Money* podcast for the past four or five years, but I really don't understand why, historically, we haven't spoken more about the relationship between mental health and spending, and self-care and spending – what that looks like and how your mentality and how you're feeling impacts the way you allocate money and spend it.

Stress spending is real. And it's not something you 'get over'. I go through it maybe once a month, so I use the SOTM Budget and Cashflow Masterclass tools to help me stay on top of my spending. If I can see everything in a really simple, easy way it helps me get back on the bandwagon really quickly instead of falling off completely.

Now that I've realised that spending is my default stress response, I use it as an opportunity to check in with myself and have a bit of self-compassion, which is a hard thing to learn, I think, if you are naturally quite hard on yourself.

Alright, last question. At the start of the episode you rated your money habits a C plus. But you're working on your emergency fund, you've got an investment, you're on top of your HECS, you're using my masterclass. Do you still think C plus represents your situation, and if so, what would it take to get a higher grade?

I think I'm a C plus this week. This week, I did some stress spending, so I think it varies.

Oh no, we don't change our grade based on that, that's too high school.

Okay. In general, maybe a B, then.

What would it take to get to an A, my friend?

I think, maybe, more consistent investing. I would like to do that once I've gotten my emergency fund to a level I'm happy with and then I think I'd be pretty pleased.

She Won the Lottery . . . Now What?

Having just turned 30, this money diarist is living the life of dreams after winning the lottery five years ago. But successfully managing a sudden windfall can be harder than it sounds, often burdened by potential liabilities, luxury lifestyle temptations and strained relationships. Having conquered these challenges, our diarist is using her win as a stepping stone to better things as she continues her career as a paramedic.

Let's start with what grade you would give your money habits from A through to F.

At the moment, I'd give myself a B, but I'm hoping I might be able to improve on that a little bit.

Tell us about your money story.

I've had a good money mindset from a young age – my dad was always lecturing me about how to be frugal and have a budget and taught me a lot about shares and investing. He even bought me some shares when I was a child. Then, when I was a poor university student, I bought a ticket online for a lotto jackpot of around $40 million. At the check out, they offered $2 charity tickets for a luxury prize home, so I popped them into my cart too – $10 worth of tickets altogether – and then forgot all about it.

Fast forward to about six weeks later – I'm studying in the uni library and I get this phone call from a private number. Hi, they said, it's Surf Lifesaving, blah, blah, blah. I'm rolling my eyes, thinking, I don't want to donate money, I'm busy trying to do an assignment, leave me alone. But then they asked me if I'd bought a ticket in such and such a draw? And I remembered the ticket.

So they asked a few more questions about it and I started to think, why are they asking all these questions? Then they asked if I owned my own house, and I was like, no, I am a student, I'm renting. By then a part of me had started thinking, what if? Maybe? But my brain was like, no, this doesn't happen to normal people! And then they said, we think you should sit down, we've got some good news for you.

At that point I started to freak out, so I went outside and sat down on a random bench at uni, and they said, congratulations, you've won a $1.3 million house in Sanctuary Cove, Queensland! My throat caught and I felt like I was going to cry. How will you celebrate? they asked. And, by the way, we'll email you the conveyances.

I've won the lottery! I think. And at the same time, I can't believe it's true! I hang up and I'm waiting for their email, refreshing every 30 seconds. While I'm waiting, I call my partner and he's like, no, you've been scammed. It's a scam. And I'm like, no, I'm pretty sure this is legit, I bought the tickets, they had my number, it all stacks up. But he's just not with the vibe, so I hang up on him.

So then I call my dad and he believes me instantly. And then I call my mum and she's just in shock. She can't even speak. She thinks I'm joking and I'm like, no mum, I wouldn't joke about this, but I can't tell her much more because the email still hasn't arrived and I can't remember any details about the house other than that it was in Sanctuary Cove.

About an hour later, I got the confirmation email with all the solicitor's details. When they'd asked me what I was going to do to celebrate, I'd said I have to go to work at the local pub in two hours. Can't you just call in sick, they'd asked, but I'd been like, no, I'm just going to go to work like normal. So I did. I just went to work as if nothing had happened.

A couple of weeks later, I flew up to Queensland for the handover. My dad and my partner at the time both came with me. We did a little tour of the house, I signed all the paperwork, then was given the keys to this amazing house in a gated estate that had two golf courses. It came fully furnished, had a barbecue and a swimming pool and its own golf buggy and golf clubs! As a student who lived elsewhere, I sold the golf buggy straight away, but initially I didn't do anything with the house. We had a few holidays up there, all my family and my partner's family came to stay.

It came with its own expenses, of course, but I wasn't sure if I'd have also to pay some tax on it because of capital gains. I got a couple of accountants' opinions, but because it was a charity and lottery, I didn't have to pay anything at that point in time – it was a prize, at the end of the day. But still, there was upkeep and rates and everything. So I started looking around for tenants, but it was actually quite hard to rent as it wasn't your average family rental. Fortunately, a neighbour had sold their house so they leased mine for about six months while they looked around for a new property. They maintained it really well, but when they found somewhere to buy they wanted to break the lease, so my parents moved in. In the end, Mum and Dad got so comfortable there that they ended up purchasing it off me. They paid its original value – so I got the money, they stayed in the house and, in future, my brother and I may inherit half each. It all worked out.

How long did you own it before you sold it to your parents?

I won it in 2018 and sold it at the end of 2021, so about three years. I was working overseas at the time. I'm a paramedic and when I finished uni I went to work for the NHS in England. So initially, the money was just sitting in my bank account. The day it got transferred across, I just couldn't believe it. I checked my bank account and there was so much money in there! I kept it in a high-interest savings account so it was making a lot of interest for a while. Then, once I came back to Australia, I had to work rural remote initially and I didn't want to buy a place out there. But once I got settled in Adelaide, where I am now, I bought a house in cash.

So you bought your house outright?! What did you pay for it? Is there any cash left?

I paid $640,000 for the house. I also paid off my HECS in one go. I had two degrees, so it was quite big, around $70,000 with all the indexation, so I paid that off.

I also bought a new car as my 12-year-old Mazda 2 was on its last legs. I got a Mitsubishi Outlander – the nice, new one. I wanted some room for pets and, I don't know, maybe kids or something one day. So I went from a tiny car to a decent-sized one.

And then also, because I'd worked in England through COVID, I hadn't got to do much travelling, which had been my main reason for going to work over there. So this year, I went on an eight-week European trip. It was a fairly big expense, but I figured I had the disposable income to cover it.

After that, I was like, okay, your treat-yourself stage is over. Time to get serious. So, last month I bought an investment property.

How old are you now?

I'm 30. I won the house when I was 25. So, other than my emergency fund, most of the remainder of the money went to the new investment. It's negatively geared at the moment, which is good for tax and things. It settles soon, so I'll look to get tenants, a nice family or something. I'm hoping to get $700 a week for it. It's a four-bedroom house near the beach in Adelaide.

So one day, there you were at uni, studying to be a paramedic – not, I imagine, for the pay but because you care – and suddenly, you find yourself financially sorted. How does it feel – is it as amazing as people might think?

Obviously I've been blessed with a big windfall, but it has come with downsides as well. My ex-partner, even though the ticket and title and everything was in my name, was under the impression that, because we were dating, it was ours, like a joint thing. I asked him to sign a binding financial agreement but he refused. He was adamant he wasn't going to sign and thought it was a sign of mistrust or that I was going leave him for someone better, basically. I tried explaining that I didn't want to leave, but that if we ever did separate, I didn't want him to take half of my things and said I would happily sign one if the tables were turned, et cetera.

Eventually we just got to a point where I realised, it wasn't going to work. We had different money backgrounds. He was a bit more of an impulse person and would just do things for a good time, whereas I'm a bit more of a frugal Fran. Fortunately, I'd set everything up so my assets were protected. Once we split, it got pretty messy and he still tried to make a claim, but luckily I could keep the house. I think us breaking up was probably a blessing in disguise.

If I ever go on a proper date with someone and we get to that stage where we're talking about finances, I'll be like, here's my binding financial agreement, sign it or go home. I'm going to have to carry it around in my purse and be like, you have to sign this if you want to stay with me or bye! I feel like, especially in this day and age, that's the way you have to be if you don't want to get taken advantage of. I'm hoping to meet someone who has the same sort of goals as me and their finances in order so we can work together, but also separately on our goals, rather than one person sort of feeding off the other person to get somewhere.

Have you lost other friends or had awkward conversations around this?

Not really lost friends, but . . . some people I told were super happy for me, like, oh, we couldn't think of someone more deserving to win. And then other people were maybe a bit jealous, I guess. If my friend won, I'd be jealous, but I'd still be happy for them.

I told a friend that I'd submitted my money story to you, and she was like, why would they use yours? You won that money. It's not like you had to budget. Literally, that's what she said. And I was like, excuse me! Obviously I was blessed to win that money, but I've used it to make more money. I haven't just been sitting on it. I have been budgeting, obviously.

Anyway, I've just decided not to mention it to anyone anymore. A couple of my close friends at work know and my boss who's got a few properties himself who's become another dad–mentor sort of person. It's a bit of a touchy subject.

She's *on the* Money

When I worked as a financial advisor, I used to specialise in inheritance and I'd deal with younger people inheriting millions of dollars. I saw so many people literally let the money drain through their fingers. They didn't have any financial literacy and had no idea what they're doing.

I had one client buy a Maserati – I think they spent around $600,000 on it. It wasn't all of their inheritance; it was actually quite a small portion of their inheritance, so go, have fun! But they didn't get insurance on it. They went to the dealership and picked a car they could drive away. Then they crashed it driving home and it was a write off. Not only did they write it off, but they wrote somebody else's car off and they had to pay for that too!

What I always hoped to see in these inheritance situations, and I do see here, is someone using their windfall as a stepping stone. To approach it like, these are the things I wanted to do anyway, I've just turbocharged it and I'm making the most of it.

So you might not have to work, but if so, what do you do and how much do you get paid?

I'm still a paramedic. I always wanted to do healthcare so I could help people. It's a great job and the pay where I work is really good – as a single person, I get a really decent wage. I still have a lot of goals to meet, so I'll be working for a while yet!

So many people I told, when I won and was working casually at uni, were like, why don't you just quit? And why bother finishing your degree? You don't have to work. And I was like, it's not enough to never work again. Plus, I *want* to be a paramedic. Even if I won $40 million, I'd still want to be a paramedic.

At the end of the day, so much of what we think we want is just material stuff. As a paramedic, I'm often reminded, that no, actually, I just want to be alive tomorrow and that's enough. Ultimately my goal is just to have enough money to live how I want to and, if I'm lucky enough to have a partner or kids or something, to set them up as well.

My work's kind of flexible but we also work quite hard. At the moment, I get about $122,000 but I'll get a pay rise in April so then I'll be on $126,000. And then, I've decided to go back to uni to get my intensive care qualifications and that should put me up to about $140,000.

I love that you get paid well as a paramedic, but I know it's a tough job. What are the downsides?

I don't know how people do it with kids. Even for myself, I never make plans after work because you're not guaranteed to finish on time. Just the other day I finished two hours late on a day shift, so it turned into a 14 hour shift. So you can't make plans to meet someone for dinner, you just have to be like, these are the days I'm at work and then these are my days off. We're quite lucky to get days off during the week so you can do your banking and things like that, which would be harder in a nine-to-five.

Gosh, a 14-hour shift. That takes stamina! What's the most common reason for a call out?

I would say chest pain or mental health or social issues, whether that's alcohol or homelessness, domestic violence. Those sorts of things are really on the increase in both young people and in the older generation, especially after COVID, I think it just hit some people really hard.

Tell me a bit more about your attitude towards money now. How do you approach money today?

I'm very fortunate to be in this position and I think I have a positive mindset towards money. I see it as a tool, a necessary thing to get by – we all need money to survive. But then I also see it as a wealth creation tool to build my future. Before winning the house, I already had that mindset, but I was just starting out. I had a budget and a plan and always wanted to use money wisely to get somewhere. When I won the house I wanted to avoid lifestyle creep and obviously I didn't go out and buy a Ferrari or something ridiculous when I had all the money.

But you were also quite financially literate because of your upbringing.

Yeah, I was lucky I had that background. And I don't think my parents would've let me do anything spontaneous with it either. There were a few dad lectures before I sold the house to them – I wasn't to go out and blow it all the next day!

You've obviously achieved a lot in your 30 years, which is very cool, but what are your big money goals? What are you currently working towards?

My big one at the moment is to pay my mortgage down so that I create enough equity that I can purchase again and just keep building up my property portfolio. And my other money goal is to keep working on my super. The super fund I'm in is a government one, so I make extra contributions on top of the mandatory one which brings the total to up around 20 per cent.

Oh that's very sexy. So how much do you have in super right now?

Only about $79,000, which I think is average for my age. I worked casual when I was at uni and doing two uni degrees obviously impacted my super and then working abroad I opted out—

I'm going to cut you off there. For women between the age of 30 and 34, the ATO states the average super balance at just over $46,000.

Oh? Well my accountant said it was average, but he's a man, so maybe he was thinking male figures!

For men in that age bracket it's just over $56,000.

Wow. Okay. I honestly have had lots of breaks from building it, though. I mean, I wasn't contributing to it when I was working abroad. So when I came back at the start of 2022, I made it a goal to contribute extra to my super and make up for that loss. I've set it on the high-growth profile, so now it's doing its thing.

Based on a figure from my dad, I'd like to get to a million dollars in my super fund. My accountant thinks it's achievable, but he said that even if I don't make it, I've got my investment portfolio sorted, so I don't need to stress about my super so much.

My long-term goal is to have an investment portfolio so I can semi-retire at 50. I still want to work after that, but on my own terms, because it's a physically demanding job. So whether that's getting rid of night shifts and only working two day shifts a week or having more flexible hours, I want to work just for enjoyment rather than financial responsibility.

So you've got your properties and your superannuation. Do you have any other investments?

I have about $5000 in shares but I've put that on the back burner while I focus on my mortgage and everything.

Tell us about the debt you're carrying at the moment.

I have quite a large mortgage, even with the money I put into it. I geared my first property using 20 per cent equity to help buy the investment. The mortgage is about $700,000, but it's a four-bedroom house near the beach and I sort of look at it as good debt, as eventually it will pay for itself and more. I just have to do the hard work on it now, so I'm quite cash poor at the moment, I guess.

Any other personal debt?

Before I went to Europe I got a credit card, but just for frequent flyer points. I pay it off every month, so I use it more like a debit card but to accrue all these points. Now that I've done Europe, I've been thinking about cancelling it as I don't really need it for points. Then again, it's just sitting there and not bothering me and I think I'm pretty responsible. I'm not going to go and max it out and then not pay it.

Next year I'm anticipating I'll have a bit of a HECS debt again, but I'm not too worried about that. So I think my debts are pretty under control at the moment. I do have debt, but it's the good kind.

She's on the Money

We talk a lot in our community about 'good debt' and 'bad debt'. By our definitions, 'good debt' is something you take on to build the wealth of future you, such as an education debt like HECS/HELP, or a mortgage on a property asset that will grow in value. Whereas 'bad debt' is used to purchase items that you don't really need and which lose value – such as cars and clothing.

Debt on these is especially bad if they're items you can't afford and which don't contribute to your income. Usually they're bought on very expensive debt too, like credit cards or buy now, pay later credit which may have very high interest rates and short repayment windows. Obviously there's a caveat when it comes to some vintage or luxury-designer goods that may increase in value over time, or maybe a car or wardrobe if you need them for your job. But even then, beware!

If you go into debt to buy things you don't really need and you can't meet the minimum repayments, it's likely you'll start accruing interest and your debt will keep growing. That is the worst kind of debt.

So tell us, what's your best money habit?

My first one is the 24-hour or 48-hour rule. Basically, if I want something I'll sleep on it and think about it. Say if I'm in Kmart, I'll randomly pick something up and be like, oh my gosh, I really want that. But then I make myself pause and put it back on the shelf. I make a note and consider whether I really need it, otherwise I could easily spend $200 on impulse purchases.

Then my other one, which I used when I bought my car, is to ask whether they have a government discount, or as a first responder, if I'm entitled to any discounts. With my car, I ended up getting a $1500 discount because they put it under their fleet pricing – I just had to show them my government pay slip. And now that I'm going to be a student again, I'll be asking for that 10 per cent student discount too!

Alright, let's flip it. What's your worst money habit?

I'd say my worst money habit is that I'm a voracious reader, so I just buy too many books. This year I've read about 135 books. I just need to calm down if there's books involved! Obviously I have three books written by a certain someone that have a special spot on my bookshelf. I lend them to friends, so they've sort of paid for themselves.

Anyway, I got a library card and found out you can put a hold on popular books. Sometimes I have to wait two or three months to get a book, but it's free! So I try and read library books rather than spending $18 on a book that I'll only read once.

Now that we've spoken, what grade would you give yourself?

I would say a B plus, or maybe an A, because I think I'm doing pretty well so far and have navigated a lot of stuff to get to this point.

Finally, on the Right Meds and on the Right Track

Content warning: this story discusses suicide and mental health.

This 31-year-old money diarist's partner took his own life in late 2021. Our diarist also has her own mental health struggles and is raising two kids on her own while studying. But she's finally on the right medication for her condition, has just started a great new job, has saved some money and received pre-approval to buy a house. Things are finally looking up!

Thanks so much for sharing your story. What grade would you give your money habits if I asked you to give yourself a grade from A through to F?

At this point I would have to say a flat C.

Alright, we'll come back to that. Can you tell us a little bit about your money story?

Growing up I had an anxiety-driven relationship with money. My mum was really frugal and we went to op shops and food banks when we needed to. My dad, on the other hand, was very frivolous. He would be in and out of work all the time. So sometimes we would be eating like kings and then at other times we'd be going to school with stale sandwiches – it was all over the place. And so, whenever I got money I just clung to it. Mum would take us to the shops and she'd ask us if we wanted anything and I'd say no.

At 15, I was diagnosed with bipolar. I moved out of home at 16 and was on medication at the time, so I was able to move interstate to work and study at the same time and just be financially independent, which was really nice. But I still held onto my money and I couldn't really save because I wasn't earning much.

Eventually, I moved back to my home town and met my partner and we ended up having two kids together. We hit it off straight away, but he had some problematic behaviours, some of which included telling me I didn't have bipolar. So I went off my medication and that's when everything went crazy. We were together for nine years and throughout those nine years I was up and down all the time. I would save money, hold onto a job, and then I'd spend it all and quit the job. It was just a mess and we were breaking up and getting back together all the time. Because of my money history, I didn't like to take money from him. I always wanted to be independent. Whenever he gave me money, there were always strings attached and I couldn't handle that. Looking back, I now realise it was financial abuse.

Yes. When money is given with strings attached and you don't feel comfortable in that situation, regardless of whether it's $5 or $500, that is financial abuse. And it's all the more heartbreaking when the person doing the abuse is the person you love, right?

Exactly. I loved him, so I justified it, but as a result, I stayed on Centrelink and didn't take a dime from him . . . but that also meant I couldn't get ahead. He had depression too, which he didn't manage well. Later on, he did admit himself to a mental health ward for a bit. When he got out, he went back to work and was earning really good money as a rope access technician, working on high-rise buildings. I don't know where the money went, but it never really came to me and the kids. Towards the end, I did get him to start paying child support. We were together, but not together all the time. It was really complicated and I think that's what comes with an abusive relationship. It's not fluid, it's all over the place.

I ended up cracking in 2021. The pressure got too much for me. I had a really bad episode and ended up in the mental ward in the public system. I had no money. I'd spent it all on who knows what, and I was at a really low point. I was told if I didn't go to the mental ward voluntarily, I'd be forced to go. So I opted to go and I stayed there for a month. My two little girls, who are seven and four, stayed with my mum and dad. My mum was very supportive during that time. The girls' dad looked after them as well and it was probably the longest time he'd consistently spent with them in a while. When I got out, that's when we had an argument and he decided to take his life. That was really hard.

I can't imagine. I'm so sorry. You know that's not your fault, right?

Yeah, I do now. I mean, it's definitely been a rollercoaster and I ended up going back into the mental ward because it was so horrific. It was really hard on both me and the girls. At that point, I couldn't go back to my rental so I moved back in with my parents.

I'm so glad to hear you had your parents during this time.

They've been amazing. I don't know what I'd do without them. They've been a huge cushion this past year and a half. After moving back in with them, I was finally prescribed some medication that was suitable. It was the first time I'd been stable in quite a while and I'd honestly forgotten what stability felt like! A few months on, I decided I wanted to get a job because my anxiety about money had just skyrocketed. I was freaking out that the girls would have nothing for their future and it was all on me. So I decided to go to work. I didn't have a degree, I didn't have much experience, but I knew I had to start somewhere. I managed to pick up a contract position that paid around $50,000 a year. I worked in that for a while, then got offered a permanent position. I've just taken up my new job and it's paying much better and my super is growing and everything's going well.

What do you do for work? How much money are you earning?

I work in human resources and I'm earning about $98,000.

That's fantastic. What about your big money goals? What are you working towards?

I recently got a pre-approval for a home loan – on the 2 per cent home loan scheme for single parents. After talking to a mortgage broker I got approved. At first I was really shocked, then excited, and then I was like, wait, hold on, I don't think I can actually service a loan just yet!

Yeah, I want to buy a house, but I also want to be able to afford an actual mortgage plus all the extras. I don't know if that's doable while still having a life outside of that.

She's *on the* Money

Reviewing your ongoing costs to hold a property *before* you buy is one of the smartest things you can do in the home-buying process.

People get so caught up in saving their deposit and really being frugal to the point of missing out on everything else. They set all their focus and intention on achieving that goal, but often don't think to conceptualise what life is going to look like when they have a mortgage.

As a home owner, it's your responsibility when the hot water system breaks down. You have to pay for property maintenance and upkeep, as well as all the rates and bills and everything that comes with owning your own home. As well as the mortgage, there are a lot of additional ongoing bills.

A lot of people come from the mindset of, oh, great, I've got pre-approval so I'm all sorted! But thinking beyond that and asking yourself how you're going to reach the point of real financial stability – how you're going to pay the bills while also properly living – is going to serve you far better in the long-term.

How much do you have in superannuation and investments?

I've got $1700 in shares and about $7600 in super. It's basically doubled since working in this new job.

That's really exciting. So tell us a little bit more about your investing journey. How did you take the first step? Why are you investing? What are you investing for?

I've been listening to the *She's on the Money* podcast for quite a while and you inspired me to take the leap and invest a little bit of money here and there to see it grow. The value has dropped a bit since purchasing, but I plan on keeping it long-term, so I'm not too worried. I believe it will always go up eventually.

For people our age, investing long-term is generally the best way to invest. Do you have any debts?

Yes, I do. I have a HECS debt which is about $26,000.

Okay, that's not too bad. What are you studying and what's your big career goal?

I'm studying for a degree in human resources (HR). I want to improve in my career and I really want to grow . . . it took me 30 years to figure out I actually like HR!

That's brilliant. Can you tell us a bit more about your mental health journey, especially about your medication and how finding the right drug has impacted your quality of life?

When I was young, I was prescribed an antidepressant because the doctors thought I had depression. That sent me into a manic episode, which is what happens if you have bipolar. So they quickly took me off that drug and put me on a different medication. Finding the right medication was life-changing, but it was trial and error. One medication gave me a head-to-toe rash and so they had to quickly take me off that, but it was the medication I really wanted. We tried the non-generic brand which turned out fine.

Tell us about the financial impact because this sounds like an expensive process with lots of different therapists and different medication changes.

Thankfully it doesn't cost me too much. I spend about $40 on medication a month. With this new job, they pay for private health insurance, so I can get that covered. I'm not really out of pocket anymore, but therapists are expensive. I've always had a mental healthcare plan, so that covers a big portion of the cost, but you're always left with a gap fee depending on the therapist you see. And then there's the long wait times. When you're having an episode, you can't really get yourself organised to see a therapist, let alone sit through the waiting time. And then, by the time the appointment comes around, you don't have the money. I somehow scraped by and managed to afford therapists, but if your mental healthcare plan runs out, you're on your own again if you can't afford it.

What does the future look like? You've gone through an insanely traumatic event and you have two kids. Where do you see yourself going next?

I want to be able to keep affording our lifestyle. I've got the girls in gymnastics and swimming and I don't want to give those things up because I want them to have everything they need and more. I've got to figure out how to balance long-term goals like buying a house, with short-term goals, like making the kids' lives as good as I can. I'm hoping to keep increasing my income and I want to finish my degree and just keep pushing.

I love this. What do you think is your best money habit?

My best money habit is probably doing all my own beauty stuff at home, and that saves me a lot.

What do you think is your biggest money win when it comes to doing stuff at home?

Probably nails and lash lifts.

And what about your worst money habit?

It's going grocery shopping without looking at the prices. As a kid, my mum used to look at every single price on the supermarket shelves and I would have to calculate the total. So now I'm pretty frivolous with my grocery shopping and spend way too much!

That's a luxury you deserve to have.

Yeah, I hope so.

At the start of our chat, I asked you to give yourself a money grade and you said a flat C. But you've told us you're providing for your kids, you've increased your income in a great new job, you're investing, you have an excellent mindset around saving and also living, and you have some really good money habits. Do you still think you're a flat C?

I have really high expectations. But assessing myself objectively, I think I'm doing really well, considering everything. If I'm being less judgemental on myself I actually think I'd like to give myself a B plus.

The Financial Side of Fertility

Let's meet a 29-year-old law student who's juggling study and working full-time in a law firm while being a part-time 'bonus mum' aka stepmum. On top of that, she's also dealing with infertility and she and her partner have spent $10,000 on IVF. That's gotta be a challenge for anyone.

First question, what would you grade your money habits?

I've given this a lot of thought and I've settled on a B minus.

Alright, can you tell us about your money story?

I grew up in a family where money was never really discussed, but it was also never really an issue. We were middle class, which I think really impacted me when I finally moved out of home and went to uni. I remember very clearly having only $20 in my bank account and wondering how was I going to pay for food. It was a really big turning point for me. I had to learn how to do a budget for the first time, but I ended up working two jobs and pulling it together.

Totally. Money's hard and you don't realise that until you're on your own with it.

Yes, exactly. Before I could always rely on my parents to bail me out when I spent my $50 paycheque from working at the chicken shop on lip gloss!

Yes! So you became an adult and you had your first $20. What happened then?

So I started uni when I was 17 and I didn't really know what I wanted to do. I decided on something that I thought would make me sound smart and employable and enrolled in journalism. On the first day of my journalism course, the lecturer stood up and said, journalism is a dying profession. You have two weeks till the census date. I suggest you consider doing something else.

I stayed on for a little bit, but fell into a bad loop of anxiety and depression and that was it for me. I took a break to focus on myself and ended up working a few different retail jobs, and then I eventually moved into the public service where I started my career as a criminal investigator.

It was through that role – doing investigations and working more in regulation – that I discovered my passion for law. So I left the public service and I'm now in a litigation team at a private law firm. I'm still in the process of getting my law degree, but I'll get there!

You said you're also a 'part-time bonus stepmum'. Tell us about that.

My stepdaughter is pretty much the coolest person in the world. I know it's kind of lame to say that, but she's so confident and funny and bubbly and she just does not let anything hold her back.

I met her dad when we were working together as investigators. It was an office romance and gorgeous. When I decided he was going to be my husband, I really sat down and thought through the whole stepmum thing. I wanted to take it really seriously because she didn't choose this and she deserves all of my effort. When I decided to commit, I jumped in feet first and it's worked out really well.

And you and your husband have been trying to become second-time parents?

Yes. But I have a fertility issue called primary ovarian failure or primary ovarian insufficiency. Essentially that means I'm perimenopausal at 29.

It's a big thing to come to terms with. We started looking at all the available procedures, like in vitro fertilisation (IVF) and intrauterine insemination (IUI), and getting all those ducks in a row because the time it takes to even get to the point of the actual fertility procedure is so long – you have to do so many tests and there are so many hurdles. We actually fell pregnant in November last year, but we miscarried at the start of the year around January.

It was tough. The minute I got a positive pregnancy test, I thought it was going to be perfect. I just thought that's how it worked – I'm healthy, I'm okay. But unfortunately that's not always the case. It's hard talking about it, but I think it's important, because if I share my load and you share yours, I know that I'm not alone and not the only one to go through this. Talking about it helped me realise that a non-viable pregnancy is not a reflection of me being a terrible mum. I think a lot of the time we blame ourselves for not doing something or doing something wrong or messing it up somehow. But often, that's not the case at all.

No, but sometimes you need someone externally to give you that reminder. So you went through three rounds of IVF and then had a miscarriage. What happened next?

Yeah, so we've already spent about $10,000 on three rounds of failed IVF. At the time, I had to travel to Sydney to access a bulk-billing IVF clinic, which halved treatment costs, but then you have to factor everything else in, like interstate travel, hotels and accommodation.

We're at the point now where we need to look at using donor conception and donor eggs. Luckily our clinic has just introduced these to their bulk-billing schedule, as it basically means doing IVF on two people: me and my donor.

You seem really positive. How have you dealt with all of it?

When I miscarried, the procedure I needed afterwards – a dilation and curettage (D&C) – was probably the single worst experience of my life. It sucked and it was horrible and it's not something I would ever, ever wish anyone to experience, but I can't change it.

The donor route isn't anyone's first choice, but they're the cards I've been dealt and there's no point being angry at my body. It's done a lot of good things for me too, to keep me safe and keep me healthy and keep me going. But it is hard.

I'm very fortunate that my cousin went through six rounds of IVF to have her little girl, so she has been an amazing support. If anyone is looking at IVF, there's a reality show called *Big Miracles*. I ended up going back and rewatching it recently and I found it a really helpful resource as well.

I'd also like to give a shout out to my therapist – she's done a lot of the heavy lifting and we really appreciate her. She's done great work.

You're on the right track and I can tell you're going to be the best mum. You said that you work in full-time litigation. What does that mean and how much do you earn?

I'm a legal secretary in a litigation practice in a private law firm and I earn about $97,000 a year. Our primary clients are Commonwealth government agencies. We represent those agencies when other parties initiate litigation against them – basically when they get sued. Yes, Victoria, some of the gossip is incredible, but I can't tell you any juicy details as I've signed an NDA!

That said, it's also really helpful because I'm in the process of getting my law degree, so being able to work full-time in a private firm in that litigation space is very cool. And all the networking, all the contacts.

Oh, I love that for you. What's your big money goal? What are you currently working towards?

Currently we have two big money goals. Our first is to save a deposit to buy our own house. And our second is to save up a bit more money so we can commence some further IVF rounds using an egg donor.

We should be able to purchase a house late next year. We're thinking around November, December. Then hopefully we'll be able to start IVF, visiting an egg donor just after that.

Do you have any investments? If so, what are they?

I'm in the process of growing my Spaceship portfolio. I've got roughly $1000 there and I've got $96,000 in super.

For almost two years now, I've been salary sacrificing into my super account which has really bumped it up. And they've just increased the cap as well, which is helpful. So I've been able to really contribute into that with the view of using some of those additional contributions to help fund our house deposit through the First Home Super Saver (FHSS) scheme.

She's *on the* Money

The FHSS scheme allows first home buyers to make voluntary contributions into their super fund to save for their first home, then withdraw those funds when the time comes to purchase their home, up to a total of $50,000.

By redirecting your income into super, you will reduce your taxable income in that year. Then, when you withdraw your money, the released amounts will be taxed at your marginal rate minus a 30 per cent offset. For the majority of the SOTM community who are on the 32.5 per cent tax rate, once we include the Medicare surcharge that means paying 4.5 per cent tax on that portion of their income.

However, before you decide this is for you, it's important to know that the scheme has strict limits and eligibility requirements. Once your money's been deposited into super, it can only be withdrawn by application and for limited reasons, so make sure you meet all the eligibility requirements. It's also important to make sure that your nominated super fund will release the money and to know about any additional fees they might charge.

So how did all that come about, did you get any help?

I sat down about 18 months ago and reviewed my whole financial situation. I looked at my super fund's performance and decided to call around and compare super funds. I spoke to a few over the phone, explaining my goal and where I want to be and once I'd found one that seemed suitable, I sat down with their financial planner who explained their scheme in further detail. Compared to my current fund, their fees were about half and they had performed better historically over the longer term, so I switched.

This process was absolutely free and it's something that most super funds offer. My fund also offers a bunch of really good resources: they do webinars, they have ebooks and you can access a free financial advisor through them a couple of times a year. They're also super easy to work with. Now I just BPAY my fees in bulk at the end of each financial year.

She's on the Money

Many super funds offer simple advice at no extra cost and it's worth using these services if you're already a paying member. You should be aware, however, that such advice can only be general in nature and can't compare products outside that fund. Nor can it be personalised to your circumstances or advise on consolidating your super or alternative investment options and products.

For a broader view of the market, both government and community organisations offer free advice on superannuation. These include the government's Financial Information Service which provides both online tools and phone consultations, and the ASIC Moneysmart website.

Money win! So you've got your Spaceship and then you've got your $97,000 in super. Let's bring down the mood: do you have any debt?

I have no consumer debt but I do have a HECS debt, which is roughly $20,000. By the time I finish my law degree it's probably going to be closer to $60,000. When I'm earning the big bucks as a partner, it'll be worth it!

It'll be fine. What do you think is your best money habit?

My best money habit is that my cashflow system is completely automated. Everything is set up, the money hits the bank accounts, then it gets transferred where it needs to go and I don't have to check my bank accounts at all.

My husband and I have different banks but we centralise through Up bank. We send our paycheques directly to our two Up accounts and from there we automatically transfer money. We send spending money to our individual bank accounts and also each transfer savings.

We also have a savings account set up for my stepdaughter so when she turns 16 she'll have $10,000. Keep in mind she's seven. But she wants to be a marine biologist and move to the beach.

And what do you think is your worst money habit?

My worst money habit is definitely dopamine seeking through spending. Especially buying bubble tea!

At the start you graded yourself a B minus but then you told us about your automated cashflow system, how you're earning $97,000 a year, and that you have these big money goals. You're already using the first home super saver scheme. You're using a superannuation advisor. Do you still feel like you're a B minus? What would it take to get to an A plus?

I think to get me to an A plus, I would like to be a bit more effective with managing my little treat spending. And getting a bit closer to some of my big goals would make me feel good too. That's when I'd be an A plus.

LIFESTYLE JOURNALLING PROMPTS

What are some other ways you could be increasing your positive cashflow – from hobbies, to investments, to savvy savings?

What is a big savings goal you have and why is it important to you? Getting deep into your emotional drivers can help you stay the course when times get tough, so write out in detail why this dream's important to you.

Sometimes it's our mental conditioning holding us back and sometimes it's our physical circumstances. Make a list of the things holding you back and ways you can actively start overcoming them. Start small and watch your success build – compound interest works in all areas of life!

If you were to dream big without limitations what's the most awesome life you could imagine for yourself? Don't hold back. Write it out in rich detail, let your dreams go wild and imagine what your perfect future could hold.

Lifestyle Money Wins

TAYLA always wanted to have pets but she wasn't in the financial position to own any. So, she started fostering kittens instead! The shelter pays for all of the food, vet appointments, toys and other supplies. She and her partner get to look after sweet little kittens with no extra costs. Not just a money win – a *life* win!

BRYDEE got her Pilates membership down by $15 per week because her local gym price-matched another studio for her. Simple and effective.

Wedding money win! **ALESSA** saved up more than $400 worth of rewards points to help fund the cost of alcohol for her wedding. What's more, she gathered up all the cans and bottles after the reception and took them to a return and earn point, earning herself $20! Can this woman save? She sure can!

SALLY started a vegetable garden and has grown more than enough broccoli to supply her weekly broccoli needs! She also grows spinach and freezes extra for curries. While gardening can be more of a hobby with mental health benefits than a serious money saver, every little bit helps.

STEPH'S IKEA bed broke, so she thought she was going to have to cough up for a new one. Instead, she picked up a great tip from our podcast – IKEA sell spare parts for their furniture. You can even order assembly parts like screws or knobs for free.

LUCY is a single mum and regularly turns to YouTube for money-saving tutorials when things break. This time, her sinks got blocked and she figured out the cause was her puppy digging rocks near the outside drain. Her partner was about to call a plumber, but she looked up how to fix it online and it only took five minutes!

CAITLIN deleted TikTok. You may not think it's a direct money win, but she is certain that getting rid of it has curbed her impulse buying things she definitely doesn't need!

SARAH discovered a future money win! She learnt about her city's Community Tool Library and she's going to go check it out. There's so many items to borrow for free including garden, kitchen and camping tools. So this is her public service announcement – see if your community has one too!

NATASHA took the extra time to shop around for her family's fortnightly meat shop. She compared two supermarkets online and saved a whopping $59!

AMBER usually purchases her dog's food online because it typically works out cheaper than buying it in-store. A pet store worker introduced her to the website 99petshops.com.au where you can look up most pet items and it automatically lists the best prices. She uses it to get the best in-store price match!

LAURA was in Melbourne for a volunteering event. She was frugal and decided to meal prep ahead of the trip because saving money was more of an important value to her than eating out. During her time in Melbourne she only spent $12 – what a go getter!

Work

While we all dream of winning the lottery, the golden ticket is actually finding a job you love *and* getting paid the big bucks – as our money diarist in the previous chapter proved! Getting to 'dream job unlocked' might take several pivots, career leaps and left-hand turns to reach, while getting paid your worth involves mastering the art of salary negotiations along with thinking creatively about how to grow your income.

As such, many of our community members run several side hustles – a great way to earn extra coin, develop skills or scratch a creative itch. Whichever way you cut the work–life pie, if you can find the optimal balance between loving what you do and making ends meet (and then some), you're well on your way to living the life dreams are made of!

A Vet With a Vision

Let's meet a driven and accomplished 27-year-old veterinarian who's really been putting in the hours, but has also been living beyond her means despite making a *six-figure* salary! She knows she needs to make some drastic changes – both in her money habits *and* her mindset. The first step? Breaking free from her spreadsheet-wielding, finance-obsessed dad.

Alright, I want to know, can you tell us about your money story?

I grew up very comfortably. Both my parents have higher degrees – Dad's got a PhD, Mum's got a tertiary degree – so we always lived extremely well. My sister and I went to good schools, not private schools, but high-performance public schools with competitive entry.

I have a twin sister, but we've taken very different paths. My vet degree took me seven years whereas my sister, a paramedic now living in London, finished her degree in three years. She moved straight over there, started making really good money and has literally been travelling the world since. We always competed against each other growing up. She has a lot of savings and travels freely, but I've always been stuck in the one place, working for a minimum wage.

Our family owns investment properties in my parents' super and they've got their own businesses. Growing up, Dad was always talking about money – he's obsessed with finances. He regularly tells me where I need to be at in my super to be able to retire comfortably and sends me spreadsheets weekly. Although perhaps not the best decision financially, it's been great for my mental health to stop being dependent on him.

It's interesting to see twins go in different ways. But we'll come back to that. How much money do you earn as a vet?

I *was* making six figures. But at the height of COVID, I took a big pay cut of about $45,000 to be a veterinary intern, which means that when you graduate you can come out as a general practitioner and get paid. The award wage is about $50,000, so not a lot. After my internship I got a residency, which means I'm now training to be a specialist and on about $90,000 a year – or about $2278 a fortnight after tax.

What are you working towards? Can you tell us a little bit about your big money goal?

I've actually split it up into short-, medium- and long-term money goals. My short-term goal is to get out of personal debt as quickly as I can and start saving.

My training program doesn't allow me to complete training in the same clinic, so I've decided to go to Queensland, Hong Kong and hopefully the UK in the next couple of years to work under some well-known vets. But all that travel is going to cost a lot of money! So all of my savings are going towards my externships.

My medium-term goal is to save a very solid emergency fund,

which I know I should have been doing earlier, but I'm paying so much debt down and the rest I'm saving. I know I'm not going to be able to save a ton of money while doing my placements, so I want to put away $15,000 to cover a few months' of expenses.

My long-term (10-year-plus) goal is to get into investment properties, like my family. But given the market at the moment and my wage and my debt from vet school, I'm not going to be able to do that anytime soon.

It'll happen in the future, though. If we make a plan, we're halfway there. Do you have any investments?

I only have my super at the moment – about $17,000 – which I think is pretty good for technically only working full-time for two years. I did have a Raiz account, but I had so much debt that I ended up taking the money straight out once it had grown a bit and used it to pay down the debt quicker because I was paying so much interest.

You mentioned that you have debts, so what exactly are they and what are they for?

I'm trying to put everything into paying my debts off. When I was working and had my six-figure salary, I paid my initial HELP loan off, which was nice. But when I went back to do my post-grad certificate it grew again, so now it's sitting at about $8600, which is not too bad, but it's still there. The original HELP loan was about $70,000.

Wow. And you paid all of that off?

I had a part scholarship and I paid part of it myself. Look, there's possibly better places I could have put my money, but it made me feel good to pay some of the debt off. At least now it's not coming out of my paycheque each and every month, so it's not the worst decision.

I also have a car loan of just over $8000 and credit card debt which I consolidated recently (a balance transfer to 0 per cent interest), so that's down to about $4000, and a fine repayment of about $1300. My workplace didn't tax me correctly last year, so I had about $1600 owing there, but it's down to about $1300 now. Taking in the loan repayments, my total debt is just under $24,000.

She's on the Money

We don't need to crucify ourselves over debt, we just need to make a plan for it. Full stop, end of story.

Dwelling on debt doesn't benefit us – feeling bad about things doesn't put us in a better position, it's just a waste of time. What we *can* do is create a budget and cashflow system that works and then put it into place.

Paying off debt is a really good lesson in discipline in savings. And the second you've paid off that $24,000 worth of debt, by using that same system, you can then create $24,000 worth of savings. You go, queen!!

Yeah, I keep a list of my debts on my computer. Once I pay off a little bit more, I knock the price down so I can visualise it and say, look, this is actually a lot smaller than it used to be!

I love that. Okay, let's move on to the next question. What's your best money habit?

I'm really good at getting the best price I can. I used to just buy stuff if I saw it and I wanted it. Nowadays, because I know how much debt I have, I actually step back and put a bit of time between my impulse and my purchases. I'll ask myself, do I *really* need this? It's one thing I think I do quite well. It saves me hundreds of dollars here and there.

And what about your worst money habit?

Putting my head in the sand, especially when it comes to groceries and little purchases. I was adding them up the other day and realised I'd spent an extra $200 over what I'd budgeted just on drinks and coffees and buying food out. We've got a pub across the road from work, so if we've had a crap day, a lot of us will be like, oh, let's go to the pub and have a drink. It adds up very quickly.

Yeah, totally. What would you grade yourself if we forced you to give yourself a money grade?

I'd probably say a C at the moment, mainly because I have the debt still, so I don't feel financially free yet. I don't want to be living week-to-week off my paycheque which I'm doing at the moment because I'm trying to pay down the debts. Once I get on top of my debts and have a bit of a savings base, then I'll increase my grade a bit. Hopefully that will happen in the next five to 10 years.

When I was little, all I wanted in life was to become a vet. Is it all that it's cracked up to be?

Yes! I love it. I love my patients and I think the work itself – the science behind it – is really interesting. But it's a very taxing job, mentally and financially. Our graduate award wage, which has dramatically improved in the last five years, is still only about $57,000. That's not a lot compared to my friends who finished medical school and earn double that. It's quite a financial strain, especially with the cost of living in Sydney and our continuing education fees – I think I spent about $7000 on those last year. But, like I said, I absolutely love it.

What are you going to specialise in?

My favourite patients are the old dogs and that's the area I'm planning to specialise in. When I work in the ER, all the old crusties are transferred to me, and my other job is in palliative care. We go around to people's houses and either put their dogs down or perform palliative care practices so they don't have to come into the clinic. It sounds depressing, but it's not.

How do you deal with that mentally?

It's all about mindset. I call it 'filling my vet cup' because most of the families are just so beautiful and so grateful. If it's a palliative care consult, we're making a plan and making the animal more comfortable and doing the most respectful thing we can. Same when it comes to euthanasia. In most cases, it's usually the family's first baby that they're putting down and they're just very appreciative.

We're an advocate for the animal. I don't mind doing it if I think it's genuinely the best decision for both the animal and the client. Money comes into it, too. Some treatments cost tens of thousands of dollars and some people just can't afford that. I don't like to see clients in the position where they have to choose between helping their pets or feeding themselves, so I try to make the process as painless and comfortable as possible.

You said that you grew up with a twin sister and that you'd always been really competitive. Can you talk us through what that's like and why you think that's the case?

My sister and I went to the same primary school and we had all the same friends. But, given the family we grew up in, with both parents being high-achieving professionals, it was always super competitive. It didn't matter whether that was extracurricular activities or school grades.

In Year 12, Dad put together a payment scheme to reward us based on what ATAR we got. He had a different amount of money that he would pay us if we got a certain mark. If we got over 99 he was going to buy us a new car, which neither of us achieved, but it's still a lot of pressure. In hindsight, that probably wasn't the best thing to put on a young person!

My sister and I ended up attending different high schools, which didn't solve a lot of issues. We are both quite academic. She went to our local selective school and I went to a different school out west – my school actually ranked better than hers. We played Dad's HSC game and I got better marks (my ATAR was higher), mostly because of the school I went to, because it was ranked higher. I don't think my sister even ended up 'qualifying' for Dad's scheme, which was just really awkward.

That's actually quite toxic behaviour!

I know. I've talked about it with my psychologist multiple times and she said it's not normal.

I'm so sorry that was your experience. Talk to us more about comparing yourself to others now you're an adult.

My sister is now in London working as a paramedic and she's making very good money, especially as they can get paid a lot of overtime. I spent more than twice the amount of time at uni and was dependent on my parents and Centrelink for ages. I really don't have any savings at the moment because of all the debts, but I can't help that. So it gets pretty awkward when my sister wants me to come and meet her in Greece, say. She tells me she's happy to pay – but then I'll owe her $5000. I just don't have the money to pay that back and I don't want to do that to her either.

A lot of my friends are teachers and nurses. They finished uni around the same time as my sister and a lot of them have bought houses now and maybe half of them are getting engaged. Some of them even have babies! I'm obviously at a very, very different point in my life. I know that it's going to be a good 10 years before I'm in that position.

It's tough to be a happy human being if you're consistently looking at other people and going, oh, I can't be happy, I don't have what they have.

I'm trying to learn how to practise self-gratitude, looking internally and saying, oh my gosh, I'm actually a really cool human. I work hard and I've paid off $70,000 worth of HELP debt on my own. You killed it, babe! That's more than a house deposit for most people.

I'm lucky that my friends and I talk very openly. I'll say stuff like, I'm very fricking broke at the moment just with the debts that I have to pay off. But sometimes they'll turn around and be like, but you're a *doctor*! So I have to explain that I'm doing big things and a residency is very hard to get, especially in the early stages of your career, blah, blah, blah. So yeah, I'm doing well, but it's hard sometimes to remind myself to think like that.

She's *on the* Money

In situations like this, it's good to reset all your values and goals. Pop some blinkers on and just focus on where you are up to and not where anyone else is up to. Put in place not only a plan to achieve your goals, but a plan to celebrate the small wins too.

What are you going to do when you pay off your $4000 worth of credit card debt – are you going to give yourself a pat on the back? As much as you feel like these are small things compared to others whom you think are doing 'better and bigger', getting your own financials in order is massive.

Each milestone is a huge deal and we need to celebrate them!

Before we wrap up, I want to know: when you get back from your international externships, what kind of jobs will you be able to take on and what does that look like for you?

I've got a nice little timeline. I do my residency. In that residency, I do my externships. When I've completed those, I become a registrar for a few years. I do lots of study, lots and lots of extra study, then I sit my fellowship exams. Eventually, I'll be a small animal internal medicine specialist, focusing on older animals.

I'm really lucky – I have some supervisors who are very keen on my ideas. I actually want to be a geriatrician for animals, which isn't really a thing yet, but I feel like it will be in the future. We do it with people, why *wouldn't* we do it with animals? Especially when we can keep them alive so much longer these days. So in five to six years, I'll hopefully be one of Australia's first animal geriatricians.

That is so wholesome and so special. But also, look at that career trajectory! That is so cool to have that clarity. You need to give yourself a bit more credit.

It's true. Sometimes I just need to step back and be like, you know what, I've actually achieved a lot in 27 years!

Owning it on OnlyFans!

Hold on tight! This money diarist is a 32-year-old single mum who's managed to buy a house, an investment property and a Land Rover – all within 12 months, without help or relying on child support! She comes from a corporate banking background and was super unhappy in her marriage. At the age of 29 she left the marriage with only $60 to her name. She began dabbling in OnlyFans and has made – wait for it – $400,000 last year! Truly epic.

Can you tell us a little bit about your money story?

I wouldn't necessarily say that I'm driven by money or that money is a priority for me. However, stability and structure is really important to me as a single mum. I didn't have that growing up and I realised quite quickly that money was the tool to help achieve that stability, not only for me but for my kids as well.

What do you do for work and how much money do you earn?

I'm a full-time OnlyFans creator and last financial year I sold over $400,000 worth of nude content.

Wow! How does it actually work? Can you break down how you generate income, because you don't just chuck up a nude picture and someone buys it, right?

The way I like to explain OnlyFans is it's like Instagram but for nudity. It costs people to follow or subscribe to my page, so that's one avenue; I make money from a subscription price. Then I charge people to talk to me, so that's another avenue. Then I make videos either of myself or with co-stars and sell that. So that's three different income streams. I also run campaigns where I want to buy this toy or this set of lingerie and ask people if they'll contribute to it, so that's another stream. OnlyFans is the umbrella and there are a lot of different streams that come under that umbrella.

Being known as a subscription service, a lot of people probably think if you earn $400,000, that must mean you have 400,000 subscribers. But that's not how it works, is it?

No. On my page, it's like a girlfriend experience, so I'm very close with my subscribers. I've actually got quite a low number of subscribers, but they spend a significant amount compared to a lot of other girls who might have 100,000 subscribers who are only spending a couple of dollars each.

What's your big money goal? What are you currently working towards?

Ever since 19, my big money goal was to buy a house. I wanted to do it all on my own and have it just in my name, and that became even more important to me when I became a single mum. I thought it would be amazing if I could do that one day, so that's why I got into this industry. I vowed to hustle hard until I bought a house. And, actually, I did buy a house in December last year! So then it was like, okay, what's next?!

So I've also just bought an investment property. My new big money goal is my retirement strategy: I want to buy one property per year, minimum, for the next eight years. The aim is to be able to retire at 40.

Incredible. And all this happened straight after you got divorced with only $60 in your bank account? You had a friend doing OnlyFans and thought, let's give it a hot crack.

Yes, I had absolutely no experience in the industry. I'm just a mum from the suburbs and I do not look anything like a porn star. I come from a banking background! My parents got divorced when I was young which was the beginning of a long road of instability for me and my siblings. When I got divorced, I looked at my two beautiful little kids and thought there was no way I was going to let them down for anyone or for anything. I don't care what society says, I'm doing this for my boys.

You sound so happy being able to provide for your family. So, tell us more about the investment property and any other investments you might have.

I put money away into super and I've played around with shares and crypto a little bit. However, they don't really fit into my risk appetite because I'm hellbent on having everything safe and secure. I think it's a really great option for some, but not for me. So most of my investments are in super and property.

Your investment outside of superannuation makes sense if you want to retire by 40, because you can't access super until retirement age, which in Australia is 65. So your property makes good sense. And, do you have any debts?

I have a mortgage of about $220,000 on a house I bought for $270,000. I was really, really lucky to get in at a great point in time as its value has risen since I bought – it's now worth about $320,000. So it's gone up about $50,000 in six months.

That is very good turnaround. You're making money basically everywhere at the moment!

I'm trying to. I want to make hay while the sun shines.

Alright, next question. I want to know what's your best money habit?

My best money habit is when I have a goal, I get obsessed with it. So when I bought this house, I just went and put in an offer, then called my broker and was like, I've just bought a house!

He asked me why I'd done that and where I was getting the deposit from. Fortunately I'd already managed to save $42,000 in about eight weeks, so I had it covered.

As soon as I set myself a goal, I work until I hit it. Like, with my investment property, I was supposed to be using the equity in my home to buy it, but then my broker said that the bank wouldn't let me do that and that I'd have to come up with $70,000 before settlement, in four weeks' time. He offered to get me out of the contract but I told him, no, that's okay, I'll find the money. And I did.

When I have a goal, I just get obsessed with it and I can't handle the thought of not reaching it. So that's kind of how I structure things, which probably isn't the best financial advice, but that's what works for me.

Okay, so what's your worst money habit?

If I don't have a goal, I'm not very good at saving money. I could have been saving this whole time towards my deposit, but although I haven't spent a lot on material things, I'm really big on experiences. So I'll take the kids for weekends away and just spend up.

Look, I always say that so long as your decisions align with your values, then that's what matters. So how would you grade your money habits?

I think a B or a C. I'm proud of what I've achieved, but I could definitely be better with more focus.

Before you were in the sex industry, what were you doing? You were a mum, you were married, but what were you doing for work?

I worked as a corporate banker. I started working in the industry at 17 and I thought I was going to do it for a couple of years and then go travelling, but I ended up staying there. It was good; I always had enough money, but I never had any extra and once I got married that got worse. I married at 22 – way too young now that I think back on it – and we just had very different attitudes to money, which is not my fault and it's not his fault. It was just different. Once we separated, it was actually really cool to have all the responsibility on me because then I could make all the decisions. I think I made more responsible decisions then because I had nobody to fall back on. No-one was coming to save me. If I didn't make things work for the kids, then they weren't going to have a roof over their heads. So that forced me into better money habits.

How much were you earning as a corporate banker?

I was on just over $100,000 a year, but I don't know where it all went. I never seemed to be able to go out for lunch or dinner or anything like that. I think it was because I had extra people to pay for and take care of. Once we separated, it was just me and the two kids and I seemed to make the money stretch further.

It sounds like you weren't on top of your cashflow at the time. How did you find going from $100,000 to over $400,000? Have you found yourself leaning on professionals to give you advice or did you learn how to do it yourself along the way?

I'm really lucky that I know a little bit from my banking experience. However, I do enlist the help of professionals. I have an investment strategist, I have a bookkeeper and I have an accountant because even though I think I know a little bit, I didn't go to university and study any of this. So I'm happy to hand the reins over to them. They do the things that they're the experts in and I do the things that I'm the expert in, which is running my business.

And was there a learning curve jumping from the lower to the higher income?

The first thing I learnt was just how useless I am at accounting. I thought I could do my own bookkeeping and my own tax return. No, I could not! I know what I'm doing with numbers, but when I had to look at company structures and things like that, it was a smart idea to get advice from someone who knew what they were doing.

She's *on the* Money

Despite having qualified as a financial advisor, I prefer to outsource my business financials to a professional who has the time, energy and effort to stay up to date on tax law and superannuation and what's going on, and making sure that my employees are paid properly.

To be honest, after doing a little bit of a cost-benefit analysis, I realised that I'm far more valuable producing content. To do the accounting would take me triple the amount of time than it takes my bookkeeper who knows it like the back of her hand.

This is a really important factor to consider. So many people, even once they do start generating money, just don't outsource. They think it's a waste of money and that they can do it all themselves. But if you want to grow, it's a mindset shift that we have to make.

I want to know a bit more about OnlyFans. As a young mum, how did you decide to switch from corporate banking and give it a crack?

I really never intended to do it long-term. Initially, I thought I'd do it for a month or so. I was going to be anonymous, clear some bills and then move on with my life. However, once the money started rolling in I was hooked. And I was also outed very early on. Somebody contacted my ex-husband, my parents, my family; they took screenshots of me and sent the images to all the school dads.

Oh, that's horrendous.

Yep. I had people contact the police, child protection, everything. It was a really hard time because I just felt like I was at a fork in the road and could either be like, okay guys, I'm sorry, I should never have done this. Or I could say, you know what? I'm going to do this and I'm going to do it for my kids.

Someone even told me I wasn't attractive and that I was fat, that I didn't know what I was doing and that I'd never make it. I just thought, you watch me, I'll make as much money as I want to because I'm so motivated by those two little people in my life. If I don't make money for them, nobody else is going to.

I always say no-one hustles like a single parent. And it really propelled me, having all that stigma and judgement. It motivated me even more to make sure that I succeeded. I've already got this reputation now. I've already got this stigma attached to me. If these people are going to shame me and call me a whore, then I'm going to be the best whore they've ever seen!

That's a good way to own it. People can be so mean. But actively trying to bring you down probably got you more publicity?

Exactly. Each to their own. I personally am not going to go out and become a mechanic, but I don't have anything against someone who does that. I'm not going to tell them they shouldn't do it, that it's a dirty and greasy job. If it makes them happy, who cares? I don't understand why it's not the same for people in the sex industry. People think that they get to have an opinion on it, when really, they don't.

Ultimately, it's your choice. There's this stereotype that if you're in the sex industry, it must be out of desperation. It must be that you're on drugs or not doing the right thing or you're a subpar human, but you're just a mum who wants to put food on the table and give your kids the best life.

Thank you. It's something I get really passionate about. I talk quite openly about the fact that I don't look like your typical porn star. I've got cellulite and stretch marks and I've got that wobbly tummy because I've had pregnancies. My body didn't bounce back, which is fine. Before I started on OnlyFans, I'd never even been to a strip club. This isn't something that I was supposed to do, but it's something that I fell into and now I wonder why was I working at the bank! Imagine how far ahead I'd be if I'd done this years ago. The stigma that's attached to it is worth the happiness I have now and it's worth what I'm able to provide for my kids. That's everything to me.

What do they think you do for work?

They think I just work on the computer. It's not something I'm ashamed of and I'm really looking forward to having that conversation with them when they're a bit older, but at the moment they're not at an age where they should know what sex or porn is or anything like that. They see that I'm working hard and sometimes in the morning I'm really tired as I can stay up until 2 am, but I can pay the school fees in full for the whole year while working from home. How lucky am I that I get to do that?

Absolutely, it makes sense.

We don't live a fancy lifestyle, but the fact that I can pay their school fees in full is huge to me. I want them to see that their single mum worked really hard and put them through private schools by herself.

That is something to be so proud of. How have you gone with the divorce? Does your ex contribute financially or are you doing this by yourself?

He does contribute financially. But that's only started in the last few months. We owned a house and when I left I tried to have this conversation with him about how we were going to settle things financially. But he just said, you're not seeing a cent. If you want to go down this road, I'll see you in court.

I had too much on my plate and couldn't go to court. So I told him to keep everything, that I just wanted the kids. I didn't get anything from the house, it's all in his name, and he kept all his super. He does see the kids now and he does contribute a little bit each month, which is cool. But I'm glad he started contributing *after* I bought my house. It was just so important for me to be able to say that I bought the house all on my own without his help.

You said earlier that your parents' divorce was the start of a lot of instability for you. What have you changed for your kids so that they don't feel the same way?

I was 10 when my parents separated. I ended up in a boarding school in the middle of nowhere at 15 which I hated. I moved out on my own at 16 and just sort of bounced around. I ended up living in something like 30 different houses. I don't have things from my childhood and I didn't want that for my boys. We've got this dream that one day we'll buy a farm, nothing big, maybe five or 10 acres. They know that if we move again, it'll only be once and only if we get a farm. It's not all that important to the boys, but it's important to me that they've got that stability.

My parents never really taught me anything about money growing up. So the lessons I've learnt, I try to pass onto the boys. My eldest said to me, I've got $100 in my Spriggy account. If I give you $100 for the new house, do I get some rent as well? Once it settles he's going to transfer me that $100. And then once the new house is built and there are tenants in there, he's going to be getting a portion of rent every single week back into his Spriggy account.

A little hustler! Look what you've taught him.

Yeah, they just started learning about banking at school and his teacher's going to put him in charge because he was the only one who asked about interest! All these things I only learnt at 29 they're learning now. I hope that by the time they're my age they'll have a lot more than I do.

I'm sure they will, given how well you're guiding them. Tell more about how you teach kids the value of money?

They've got the Spriggy app on their iPads so they can see what their bank balance is. They don't get pocket money. If they want money, they have to come to me and say, hey Mum, I want to earn money for *Minecraft* or whatever. My youngest wrote out a list of jobs he'll do for money and put it on the fridge. Once he's done a job, I transfer the money across to his Spriggy account.

I try to let them make mistakes along the way. My youngest always just wants to go and buy lollies. His brother has that $100 he's putting into the investment property and my youngest says it isn't fair, so I remind him it's because he always spends his money on lollies!

I think it's about putting the responsibility onto them, but also helping them make good decisions and supporting them when they make bad ones. I try to have open conversations with them about money. I think we need to expose them to money and make them realise that money is real and that we all need to be held accountable.

I love that so much. You sound like you are such a good mum.

I have no idea if it's going to work out!

No, but it's more about the care and the love and the reason you do things. It's all about purpose. It's not necessarily right or wrong. There's actually no right or wrong when it comes to money stories and how people learn and what they should and shouldn't know. It seems like you're doing really well.

I hope so. I want to teach my kids the new money habits that I've learnt over the past few years. Then hopefully it'll start something in them. I don't really care if I'm rich or not, I just want to be happy and secure, so hopefully the money I'm earning can help with that. Then it's all about instilling those values into the kids.

Riding the Redundancy Rollercoaster and Ruling

This 35-year-old money diarist grew up in a family where money was tight and the cause of most arguments, after her dad got injured at work. Fast forward to now, and she's married, owns a house with a separate Airbnb dwelling and is saving for another investment property. But this turnaround has not been without its challenges. She and her husband found huge structural issues with their home and then she got made redundant; not once, but twice. Will the curveballs ever stop?

What grade would you give your money habits?

I'd say I'm a B.

Can you tell us a little bit more about your money story?

I love money! I love the freedom and the independence that it can bring, but . . . I grew up with a scarcity mindset. It's definitely still there and is something I'm trying to work through; I'm trying to focus on having more of an abundance mindset. I am definitely of the belief that money can always be replaced and it can be earnt, but I also get very attached to my money and how I spend it.

What was it like growing up with a mum who had to work two jobs to support the family?

It was tough. My dad was injured so he couldn't work. He started studying but also spent a lot of time just unable to move in bed, so mum had to look after both of us kids, and him, as well as working two jobs that didn't clash with the school runs. We didn't have much money and, although I don't feel I missed out, I was aware that my stuff wasn't as good as the other kids'. I was embarrassed about the cheap food brands I had in my lunchbox and that kids didn't want to swap their chips with mine.

Choosing home brands is such a smart money-saving hack, but it's definitely one of those things that affects your self-identity growing up. Did things change as you got older?

Yes, definitely. By the time I was in my teens, my dad had managed to get a degree. He was teaching and things changed pretty dramatically. Now he's doing so well, but he still has lots of issues with his injury and has to spend a lot of time resting. He still has a scarcity mindset and is very tight with his money.

Do you think that was ingrained by his upbringing or developed following his injury?

My grandfather was a gambler and drank a lot and he'd often spend all of his week's earnings before the family had chance to buy food. So I think it definitely stemmed from not having money growing up.

Well you've certainly turned things around in your own life – where do you think your money mindset is coming from, then?

I think there's three parts to it:

The first part is that my mum always told us to go to uni and get a good job, not do the dead-end jobs she had to. I did go to uni, but dropped out after a few months.

The second part is that I've always been fiercely independent. I've always wanted to earn my own money and work from a young age and didn't really want help from anybody.

And the third part is that when I first moved to Australia as a backpacker I got handed an amazing opportunity to manage, then own a business. It was a husband-and-wife business and she didn't want to be part of it anymore, so she started teaching me how to run it. Then they went through an awful time getting divorced and she suggested I take over the business and run it 50/50 with her husband. She wanted him to be able to continue to earn money and be around for his kids. I was scared to take it on, so I talked to my older brother. He said, we can do anything we put our minds to – think of what an opportunity this could be!

Those are the three things that have really shaped my mindset towards money.

She's *on the* Money

We talk so much about money mindsets in our community because, subconsciously, they dictate our money behaviour. The first step in changing your money mindset is becoming aware of it, by examining your inherited stories and beliefs.

When doing so it's quite common to have this lightbulb moment of realising that some of the ideas you absorbed from your upbringing – family, media, community – may not be serving you. Unfortunately, changing them can be quite hard, because it means deliberately choosing to think and behave differently from those around you.

If you grew up without much money, you may have developed a scarcity mindset, for example, but in order to grow your wealth, you'll want to transform that into more of an abundance mindset. In doing so, you may meet resistance from people who continue to live with the mindsets that defined you growing up.

While it's important to recognise that each person is on their own journey, if you want to change your future, it starts with changing your belief system and the supporting behaviours around that. No doubt that takes strength and courage, but when you do back yourself, you can create amazing opportunities for yourself.

What an opportunity! You come to Australia as a backpacker and get offered an entire business?!

Yeah, it was crazy. I definitely got thrown in the deep end. It was both exciting and very scary, but she was my mentor and there to help me with anything really big and hard and confusing.

But knowing what she was going through with the divorce, I really didn't want to lean on her too much unless it was absolutely necessary.

Are you still involved in that business?

No. I ran it for about 10 years, but as an entertainment business, COVID had a big impact on it. I'd been ready for a change for a long time before that and COVID gave me the opportunity to move on. We'd planned a year of events in advance, so there was never really a good time to step away, but obviously COVID meant lots of events were cancelled. JobKeeper payments meant I had some money coming in and I was able to bring someone else on to take on the manager role. I eventually sold the business to my business partner. He owns it completely now.

What do you now do for work and how much money are you earning?

I'm now an operations support manager for a not-for-profit organisation. I earn about $90,000 plus super, but working for a not-for-profit, I get to salary sacrifice part of my income which effectively gives me more take-home pay because of the tax benefits.

Can you tell us a bit more about how that works and how you've structured it?

I get around $611 a fortnight paid against my mortgage and a $2650 annual meals and entertainment card which I use whenever we're eating out. This is paid in pre-tax dollars, so my taxable income is reduced. It puts me about $3000 ahead.

Would you typically have spent that or do you think it actually forces you to go out and have date nights and stuff like that?

I'm still working it out as I've yet to experience it across a whole year. I was only in the job for about four months of the last tax year, so I could claim that whole amount over that four months. I was getting about $300 a fortnight towards food and meals and about $1700 a fortnight towards my mortgage, so last year was great. It's about $200 a week less now, but it's still great as it goes towards savings and we used the dining card to help cater our wedding.

What did your wedding end up costing?

We're both from the UK so our family is largely based there. My husband's parents, auntie and uncle were visiting and we didn't want to make them come out again, so we thought, let's just do it while they're here! So my parents flew out as well. We kept it really small, 34 guests, which definitely helped keep the costs down. It cost about $18,000 exclusive of the travel costs.

That is such a reasonable price for a wedding these days.

Initially I wanted to do it for $10,000 but realised very quickly, that wasn't possible. We had all the main things we really wanted and it went really well.

What blew out the most?

The venue. We were going to just get married on the beach, then hire out the restaurant and have dinner and drinks there. But then we came across a venue that was right on the beach. It was a lot more expensive, but I fell in love with it and it just felt like the right thing to do.

Love it. What's your big money goal at the moment?

We have an Airbnb at the property we live in now. It's a separate dwelling and we would like to buy another Airbnb. That's been the goal for a while. We want to buy one in Queensland because eventually we'll move back there. We're trying to figure out how much the work on the house is going to cost, how much we've got available and how long it's going to take us to be able to do that. But the second goal is that I am starting a business.

Oh my gosh, of course you are. Like you didn't have enough on!

I tried to start a business mid-last year and got made redundant and so decided to find another job and get back on my feet. Then we got engaged and married and all that stuff happened. But I'm finally back to having time to think about the business now and we're working on finalising the website. The plan is to eventually replace my income with my new business, or at least be able to work on that three days a week while I continue with my current employer a couple of days a week.

How exciting. Obviously starting a business is a really big undertaking. What are your main motivations for this? You said replacing your income; is it because you want more flexibility? Is it so you can travel? Is it so you can start a family?

It's all of the above. Before COVID, we wanted to go and live in Asia for a few months. My partner has a business as well, and I was working in my entertainment business, so we could have just done it. We're definitely adventurous. And I'd still love to do that one day. When COVID hit, we built a campervan and travelled Australia for a while, but it was a complete disaster. My husband's amazing, but he doesn't have any background or skills in building campervans. He just YouTubes and figures stuff out! He found it really difficult that I wasn't as invested or had as much energy for the build as he did, and then it took way longer than we wanted it to, so it became really, really hard. And then we set off much later than expected, so it was much hotter than expected and the dog hated it. The campervan was small and he kept hitting himself and he just didn't want to be inside. He wanted to be outside all the time but it was too hot, so it just wasn't what we envisioned it to be.

It didn't really satisfy that itch of being away from home and doing exciting new things every day. So starting this business is one way to get that sensation. On the other hand, we want to start a family and I wondered if I should just focus on the business when I'm on maternity leave. But then I thought I'd just build it up slowly. My husband's happy to step in and help manage things if I'm on maternity leave.

You are so adventurous! Tell us a bit more about how much it actually cost to build a campervan and set off around Australia. It's probably a lot of people's dream.

We bought the van for about $20,000 and spent about $18,000 fitting it out. We were still working on it once we got on the road because our rental place had come to an end and we had to move out before it was completely ready. We were still adding shelves and trying to have all these little nooks and crannies where we could store the things we needed. The plan was to make it stealthy so that we could be wherever we wanted to be and not have to pay to stay somewhere every night.

But we got nervous about just parking outside somebody's house and sleeping there. So we ended up staying in campsites most of the time. We were heading to North Queensland, but left in October or November, so by the time we got up there it was way too hot and humid to stay in the van. And, as I said, the dog just really wasn't happy! So we ended up staying in cabins at campsites that were pet friendly – but that ended up being more expensive! I was so excited about the money wins that I would get from not having to pay rent and how much would we save and all of that stuff. But it didn't quite work out like that.

Did you have fun at least some of the time?

We did have some fun, but yeah, it's hard to travel with pets because you can't really leave them. You constantly have to have somebody with them. It really limits what you can do. But I don't regret it. We learnt a lot and we went through a really hard time, but we got through it and we got married after all that.

If you can live in a van with somebody and with a dog who doesn't want to be there and still want to marry the person, I think you're marrying the right person!

Definitely.

So it sounds like maybe the van wasn't the best investment. Did you sell it?

We used credit cards to pay for it and managed to pay them all off, leaving us an asset which we sold for about $42,000. By the time we'd taken all the costs into consideration, we didn't really make anything; we'd spent a lot of our time fitting it out, but we didn't lose anything, either. Selling it gave us a good chunk of money and I sold my house around the same time, so that helped us buy the house we now live in.

How cool. So the next question I have for you is do you have any other investments?

Yes, I partly own a house back in the UK with my parents. Like I said, my dad is now doing much better. His business is going really, really well. So he bought the house that our house backs onto so he can look out the window and see the house he's bought!

I own a fifth of the house. The money I get from that, which is about £100 a month, just sits in the account and builds up and we use it as our spending money whenever we go back to the UK to visit. We have to pay for our flights, but then when we are there we pretty much have all of our spending money covered.

How good. Tell us about your Airbnb.

We bought this property that had a converted two-storey garage. It has a bedroom, a bathroom, a living area, a kitchen, and a separate driveway with parking. It's really, really nice; cute and very bright. We live in the Hills area so there are lots of trees and greenery, and it does really well. We have guests staying, on average, four or five nights a month. We earn about $4000 a month from it, sometimes more. Over the Christmas period it can be up to $7000 a month.

What are your mortgage repayments?

We have a split loan. There's $600,000 that's fixed which is about $725 a week. Then a separate portion, which was $100,000, but since we had to re-mortgage to fix the structural issues it's now nearly $200,000. We pay about $200 a week back on that. In total we're paying about $900 a week.

You're making more on your Airbnb than you are paying down on your mortgage. Did you think when you bought the property that's what would happen or was it a bit of a calculated risk?

We were quite confident. We thought we'd be able to cover our mortgage costs, but there are still expenses, so it's not money that's going into our pocket. We still have to pay tax, we've got a cleaner, and we buy breakfast supplies and put nice things in there so it feels really welcoming and homely. So there are costs on top of our mortgage. But we have friends who did a similar thing and we looked at how well they were doing, getting three or four nights booked a week, which made us confident we'd at least earn our mortgage. It was a lot less when we first moved here too, with interest rates the way they were and before we re-mortgaged.

So you've got $600,000 fixed and $200,000 variable as a split loan facility. Do you have any other debts?

No other debts, but a few other investments.

Tell us more about those.

I have a Raiz account, which I've had for a few years now, and we've got about $3600 there. A month ago I started a Sharesies account and I've got about $700 in there at the moment. I was putting in $100 a fortnight, but I'm going to increase that.

At one point I took a risk and got some crypto. We thought we'd put in an amount we wouldn't mind losing and I think the maximum we could do was $360. Immediately after we bought, it started plummeting. I haven't looked at it since, but that was probably two years ago, so I have no idea where it's at.

So of the current shares, how did you pick your investments and what was your selection criteria?

I'd wanted to do it for a long time and I'd decided that weekend that I was going to spend time setting up investments. I went to a café and sat there and it was overwhelming at the start. There was lots to do, but listening to the *She's on the Money* podcasts really helped.

I tried not to worry too much about what I was choosing, I just wanted to get in and start learning. I felt that supermarkets and banks were really solid investments so I chose a supermarket, a bank, a farming company that I recognised, and two others that I can't think of now. But I looked at the five-year history and ensured that they'd been increasing over that period.

Do you have any other debts apart from the $800,000 in loans?

No, nothing.

What do you think is your best money habit?

At the moment I'd say my best money habit has been avoiding buying new items wherever possible. We have some amazing pre-loved shops in this area. People sell clothes they don't want anymore – they're usually brand labels and are in great condition. I can't remember the last time I bought something new.

And also things like furniture. When we moved here, we got a lot of stuff off Facebook Marketplace. There are some amazing Facebook groups where people give things away for free. I'm really enjoying the community feel of that.

And what about your worst money habit?

I have a tendency to want to earn money off anything possible. When we bought this house, it had the separate space to Airbnb, but I'm now thinking of turning the whole downstairs area in our main house into an Airbnb as well. It's just me and my husband, and it's quite a big place for two of us, so I'm thinking either that, or turn it into a beauty salon or something that I can make money from. Before I got married, I was always renting houses and always had spare rooms and I'd Airbnb them. I'd give up my room with the ensuite and move all my stuff out to be able to house somebody in there so they could have a better experience and I could earn $20 more a night. I definitely still look for those kinds of opportunities.

After all you've told us I cannot believe you still think your money grade is a B. What would it take for you to give yourself an A?

There's still a lot that I want to achieve. My biggest money goal is to not have to work. I'd love to have enough properties and investments to be able to choose to work because I want to contribute to society or because I love what I do. But it would take lots more investments and lots more properties to get myself to that A and have the freedom to go and live in Asia if I want to. But I'll get there!

From Centrelink to a Six-figure Business

This is a cracking story from a 22-year-old money diarist. At the age of 18, she relied on Centrelink and borrowing money from friends and family to make ends meet. Just four years later, she's graduated, owns her own home, runs a six-figure hospitality business and does some freelance copywriting on the side. Oh, and she's carrying very little debt! What. A. Queen.

I'm excited to hear about your money story. I feel like you have had an ultimate glow-up! So, let's start from the very beginning.

My parents split up when I was very young. I was living with my mum, a single working parent doing her best. My dad remarried and had to support a family of five. It's safe to say that on both sides of the family we weren't very rich. I remember being six years old and seeing my dad and stepmum counting out 5 cent pieces to go and buy milk. They would tell us we were broke, which, looking back, is a pretty negative attitude, but I guess they were keeping it real. We learnt the value of money from a young age, but we weren't really taught how to save or how to handle money, because we never really had any. My mum's a super hard worker and Dad is too, but they were surrounded by tough circumstances and couldn't seem to find their way out.

Personally, I see money as a tool. It's not about how much you have, it's about what you're able to do with it. And that's always been my goal: to just be able to do the things I want to do and feel safe doing those things.

What do you do for work and how much money do you earn?

Almost exactly a year ago, I opened a café. I did that while I was studying full-time and working another job to pay my bills. When it opened, I worked full-time in the business, but now I just manage it. I also freelance in the social media copywriting business that my partner and I started, which has about 10 clients. Recently, I became a marketing executive for a charity, which is a fairly new role. I love it. I'm really happy there and hopefully it will turn into a full-time position later in the year. I also do some babysitting and nannying on the side when I have time. I added up my income the other day and it was just over $110,000 annually.

Oh. My. Gosh. Seriously, when do you have time for all that?!

It's definitely a case of juggling. I do freelancing work on my laptop while the kids are asleep. And when I worked full-time in the café, I could also study online.

Yeah, okay, that makes a little bit more sense. I guess you're working towards some big money goals – what are they?

My big goal is to fill all my savings accounts – I have 12 and want to meet my savings goals for all of those, which, excluding the car account, comes to just over $20,000. I'm getting there! In the longer term, my partner and I want to invest in some more property. We currently own our home and we're hoping to move from here and then turn it into an investment property. Before we invest in more property, our shared goal is to get a pool. We live in Queensland and it's very hot!

Let us know when it's done because we'll come visit! Can you tell us about the investments you have?

Using a more broad description of investment, I've obviously invested a lot of money into the café, which is definitely paying off. Apart from that, I've got $8000 in crypto. Most of that was bought for me by my dad.

Really interesting choice, Dad!

Yep. He actually got himself out of his pickle by investing in crypto. He's passionate about it and gave all of his children thousands of dollars' worth. My uncle's on the same train, so he's also given me some cryptocurrency. I've also got $2000 in an ETF through Vanguard, about $1000 in Spaceship, and a couple of hundred in Raiz as well. I would like to do more investing, but it's not my priority right now. I also pay extra into my super.

You're literally a wizard. There's no way you're 22. Do people sometimes say that you're an old soul?

Yeah, I've heard that.

Tell us about what debts you have.

I have a mortgage which is about $300,000. And also I have a HECS debt, which is about $20,000, the last time I checked. Today is Tuesday, which means my shop's credit card probably has about $700 on it because we do all the ordering at the start of the week and then I pay off the balance at the end of the week.

That's a queen-behaviour cashflow tool. Especially as I imagine you're getting good points with the amount of money that you spend through the café?

Oh my goodness, I have enough points to go on a round-the-world trip.

What? Wow.

Yeah, it's amazing. We have so much money going through the business and the card has all sorts of bonuses. So I'm just trying to use that as a tool and I pay it off at the end of every week. I'm trying to be responsible. And my accountant will get very angry at me if I use it for personal expenses.

What is your best money habit?

I actually struggle with this because I don't know if it's imposter syndrome or if it's true, but I feel like I don't necessarily have any good money habits. I'm just a really, really hard worker. If I want something, I will find a way to make that money so I can have what I want as opposed to me being a really good saver. I will find the work, I will find the time to babysit or find another client or I'll go and clean someone's house. I can always find a way to get the money that I want.

Being a hard worker is a really good habit! Rather than just using buy now, pay later or racking up more debt. What about your worst money habit?

I'm a bit chaotic and I've never been able to stick to a budget. I've tried so many budgeting tools, but I don't seem to have the discipline. I'm always transferring money out of my savings accounts. Even if I have enough in my spending accounts for my usual expenses, I'll just transfer it out and make an online order or go out for dinner or shout my friends, which is another bad habit. I mean, it's a good habit in terms of me being a nice person but . . . I'm very generous, always spending on other people, always offering to pay for dinner, buying gifts. I think my love language is giving.

She's *on the* Money

Being generous and spending on others is fine, so long as you have a good budgeting cashflow system. I've worked out, over the last few years, what my average spend is on those sorts of things and I make sure those expenses are part of my outgoings.

It's not necessarily about creating a rigid budget that you have to stick to, rather, tracking what goes into and out of your account. It's not saying, oh my gosh, this month I have an extra hundred dollars to spend on my friends and family. It's about asking yourself, exactly how much do I spend over the year?

More often than not, when your love language is gift giving, you don't really know because your weekly spend on such things is so variable. So it's nice to have worked that out – to know that, on average, you spend about $100 a month on this or $200 a month on that.

It's not necessarily about budgeting in the traditional sense where people set a fixed spending amount and feel really restricted, but rather, being aware of your spending behaviours and making decisions in line with your values.

In this scenario, it's important to understand the difference between a cashflow plan and a traditional budget. Traditionally, people would say, oh, my grocery budget's $50 this week, and force themselves to stick to that. With this approach, you keep a figure in mind that's typical of your average spend, and that allows you to be more flexible month to month.

What grade would you give yourself if we forced you to give your money habits a grade?

I'd give myself a B minus, but it's probably a B. I feel like there's so much I want to work on. I have a good income, I have the opportunity to make money, I have a stable place to live and my income is stable. I have so many tools to do amazing things with my money for my future, but I feel like I'm just not doing them. I have a fair way to go, but I think I'm on the right track.

You certainly are. One of the first things we learnt about you was that your family's money mindset is very different to yours. How did you get here? How did you change?

I met my partner! (Sorry, everybody, you can't have him!) I met him at uni when I was 19 and he was just so responsible. He had his savings account, he had his emergency fund investments, the lot!

And was he 19 as well?

He was 21, so a little bit older. When I met him I hadn't realised that people our age could actually do that, actually be financially savvy. He got me to read *The Barefoot Investor* – which I didn't finish – but I read the bit about the buckets and that started the shift in me. I can't say I stuck to it, but it definitely got me thinking more about money. It also got me saving for the emergency fund, which I think is the first big step.

That's the biggest step anybody can make regardless of their financial situation – having an emergency fund, so that if an expense pops up, you can pay for it. Around 60 per cent of Australians don't have cash on hand if something unforeseen happens. But tell us more about your café – opening a café is not a linear jump for someone studying marketing!

I was working in hospitality at the time and driving 40 minutes to open up the café at 6 am. I loved it, even though it was pretty tiring. Then my mum and stepdad decided they wanted to open a record store. They found some amazing premises near where we live which included a little café space already set up inside. They asked me if I wanted to open a business there or if I would manage the business if they did. At first I couldn't even imagine doing it. I was studying, I had a mortgage; there was no way I was going to open a business. But then I thought about it more and – you only live once, right? So why not? I have an amazing partner who would support me through anything. I have the ability to work another job, so why not just do it? So I just did it.

It cost me about $10,000 and a million hours to open the café. I sourced everything second-hand. I really wanted to do that from a sustainability point of view and obviously from a monetary point of view as well. For the first seven months, it was just me working there every day. I was exhausted. I was still studying full-time, but obviously it was during COVID, so I was studying online. But then I got to the point where I could hire one staff member and then another and then another, and now it's fully staffed.

And you're thriving.

Yes, it was a really amazing journey and I'm really grateful to have had the opportunity. It's definitely the best thing I've ever done in my life. There was a lot of behind-the-scenes work initially, but now I would say it's almost passive income. I get about $700 a week just coming in from that without me having to work there, which is the best feeling.

And it's a business that you can build up and nurture and potentially sell on one day. How do you juggle all of that backend admin with your current full-time marketing role plus your freelance work as well?

A lot of it is done on the couch at night. I also go to the blood bank every two weeks to give plasma and that takes about two hours. So that's my time where there's no-one there to distract me. I just knuckle down. I do the pays, I do the rostering, I do any ordering, I pay any invoices. I really try and just use that time to smash it out for the fortnight.

What a clever way to use that time and an incredible testament to your mentality.

I mean, I could just be sitting there watching TV, but instead I'm trying to find any extra time where I can. Like, when I was studying, I would be cooking dinner and I'd have my lectures on. I find that being busy helps me manage my time better.

How's your mental health with all of that?

It definitely comes and goes in waves. I have my struggles, we all have our struggles, and sometimes it all is a bit much. I'm a bit of a crier! About once a month it'll all seem too much. When I get burnt out and overwhelmed, it's a case of stepping back from things that I don't need to be doing. So I'll step back from doing some extra work on the copywriting business, or I'll stop going to the gym for a couple of days, or if I've committed to doing some extra stuff for the café, I'll just step back from that and have a bit of a reset, watch some TV and relax. Then I can come back refreshed.

It's the café's first birthday in a couple of weeks, so I've been doing a lot of reflecting. I can't quite believe how I was managing it at the start. Remembering that gives me a lot of strength and it really motivates me to keep going. My past self would be so proud of the fact that I'm no longer having to get up at 5 am to go to work there. I'm a big fan of doing things for my past self to make her proud.

I want to talk about your marketing role. It's not common for someone to step out of uni and then jump straight into a role that pays so well. Did you negotiate your salary? How did you come across this job?

When I was in uni, I was freelancing for a copywriting agency and the company I now work for was one of their clients. So I was familiar with the business and had already done some work for them. Unfortunately, I was unable to continue my job with that copywriting agency. A while later, I saw this role come up, but they wanted someone with five years' experience. I didn't think I was qualified, but I wasn't desperate either, so I had nothing to lose and decided to apply anyway. I had an interview and then my boss flew up from Sydney so we could properly meet and it was just amazing. We got along so well. I was obviously lucky as I only had about a year's experience but she was happy for me to start.

When it came to salary, I was absolutely shocked. I'd assumed that because I wasn't meeting all the requirements, I wasn't going to get paid the salary they'd advertised. But when she told me I would be, I was absolutely gobsmacked. I was super happy with it, but again, I weighed everything up and I did negotiate it to be a little bit higher because I had to let a couple of my freelancing clients go, and so I just wanted to balance that for myself. It was obviously a bit of a risk but they were happy for me to negotiate. Once I'm off probation, which will be next month, we've agreed on a pay rise. I think it was just a matter of not being scared and just going for it. The worst thing that could happen was that they'd say no, which was the point I was already at. So really, I had nothing to lose!

Where did you find your audacity?

I was definitely inspired by She's on the Money!

The last question I want to ask you is if someone's at uni and thinking of starting a side hustle but is terrified, what do you think they should be doing?

Make sure you're surrounded by people who will support you, not necessarily financially, but who will lift you up and give you the mental and emotional support you need. If you have someone who will catch you if you fall, that's also really helpful. I was freelancing at the time I started the café and I made sure to continue doing that, to keep the money coming in. I made sure that my expenses could be covered. Whether that's Centrelink or another job or parents or whatever, I made sure that my bills would be paid and then I just went for it. If the business failed, I still had experience in hospitality. I could get another job. If you try and if you're passionate and if you really work hard, it's likely to pay off. So yeah, that's what I'd say. Make sure that you are supported and you're comfortable and then just take the leap and do it!

Sheep, Surrogacy and the $200,000 Side Hustle

This money diarist grew up on a drought-stricken farm and was always taught that money was tight and things were tough. Mainly because they were! As a kid, it made him understandably anxious. Now 30, he's turned the tables and is a successful farmer with various lucrative side hustles. Even better, he and his partner are currently going through the surrogacy process to have a baby!

Okay, let's start as we always do: what grade would you give your money habits if I asked you to give them a grade from A through to F?

I've given this a lot of thought and I think, with the investments I've made in my own education with finance and everything, I'd be comfortable giving myself an A.

Great! Can you tell us a bit more about your money story?

It all stems back to my parents splitting up when I was about five. I don't really remember anything about money before then, but after they split, Mum went to TAFE and got educated and started again from basically nothing. She rented for ages until she was eventually able to afford to buy her first house. It was such a big milestone and I remember really noticing that. She was my role model growing up.

In my teenage years, both my parents remarried and I lived between Mum's and Dad's each week. Throughout those years, we went through a decade-long drought. Droughts happen on the land and you prepare for them, but 10 years is a long time to be living on minimal income.

So I guess that made me anxious about money. I was already an anxious kid growing up – I never did school sports or went on school camps or anything like that. Even into my adulthood, I couldn't go into shops or do the grocery shopping. I could manage little trips, but there were a couple of times when I got the trolley full, then had to ditch it and run out of the supermarket because I couldn't go through the checkout, which is a little bit embarrassing.

I guess it's all part of the journey. I'm grateful for all those hurdles I went through. It shaped the person I am with money now and I'm really thankful for that. I often used to wonder what it'd be like if my parents got back together, but they weren't happy, so everything probably happened for the best.

It finally felt like things had settled when each of them remarried, but then, when I was 23, we lost our home on the family farm to a fire. It was such a massive thing for me to deal with. I had no control of my anxiety or depression at that stage and I really hit rock bottom.

My dad and grandparents gave me the task of being in charge of the rebuild. I didn't think I could do it, it was such a big thing for me because, at that stage, I couldn't walk into the shops and pick out stuff, let alone walk into a tile shop or anything like that. But they really pushed me. I'm glad they did because it taught me how to control my anxiety and understand all those different feelings I was having. And I got some help from the doctor and that was a big turning point.

I love it. So tell us about life today. You're a farmer, you have investments and shares and you're in a beautiful relationship. And you're going through the surrogacy process!

It's amazing to think how far I've come. I've run a mental health organisation and that sort of pushed my boundaries a bit more. And then I met my partner, now husband. He brings out the best in me and has helped me flourish. We really lean on each other. We both have our things that we struggle with, but we lean on each other in those times and get through it.

And yes, now we're about to have a baby. We've gone through the whole surrogacy thing which was about two years in the making. We found a surrogate about 12 months ago, which happens to be my partner's cousin, and we're very thankful that we found someone so close.

Now we're going through the quarantine stage. We've had the embryos frozen and now have to wait three months and then we can get them tested again. After that, we can put them in.

Fantastic, congratulations. Now, we know you're a farmer, but you also have investments and shares. Tell us exactly what you do for work and how much money you earn.

My partner and I have the exact same job, which is working on his family farm. We each earn $44,000 per annum from that, with super and tax on top. So, that's our main job, and then we also do all the marketing for the farm and I do the finances and all the budgets with my partner's mum, so that's really cool.

We also have a few side hustles. We recently purchased another farm, which we had to go over the top to buy because it's a massive thing and it's not easy to get the money from the bank.

I can imagine. How much does a farm cost?

It cost us about $800,000. It was a really rundown farm of about 400 acres. We run cows and calves and from those calves we'll earn about $40,000 this year. Last year we earnt about $60,000 because of the price fluctuations. We also do some photography and videography work in the stud stock industry with sheep and cattle. We film and take photos and then the owners can sell the animals online. It's all about the genetics and that type of thing. We'll make between $80,000 and $100,000 from that this year.

And then, we have stud border collie work dogs. Each year we'll have one litter, occasionally we'll have two depending on what's happening. But we get about $20,000 from that per year.

So in total we make between $200,000 to $300,000 a year. The farm income is quite low, but we get a lot of bonuses with that and the flexibility to do off-farm work as well.

You have the same job as your partner. Did you meet him at work? Is that how you fell in love?

No, I ran a mental health organisation and I met him through that, so that's how it all started. I started by helping the organisation out with their marketing – I had a camera and then from there they offered me a job.

And a husband, it seems!

Yes. And so I left my family farm, which was a huge thing, but I wouldn't change it for the world. Even though it was a big thing moving from my family farm, I've come to my husband's family farm and it is absolutely amazing. I love working here.

What are your big money goals at the moment?

Number one is the baby. Doing surrogacy isn't cheap and we've spent about $23,000 on that so far.

We're not allowed to pay our surrogate as commercial surrogacy is illegal in most states in Australia, but as an altruistic surrogacy you do cover all the surrogate's expenses. There's a lot of blood tests and stuff at the start. And then my sister donated the eggs, so that whole process is included in that figure as well. That's pretty much everything: $23,000 to date, which is up until the embryos were frozen. We've still got to pay for the surrogacy process. So we've allowed about $30,000 altogether, but I'm not sure if it's going to blow out or not. You don't know how many times you'll have to do it and there are so many what ifs. We've got spare money ready just in case.

After that, the next thing is that we've started building a house on the farm and we want to pay as much as possible off that. Our huge money goal that we always dream of is having an investment portfolio which we'd use to help friends and family in times of need.

You're the best human I've ever met!

I've got a couple of cousins that are going through some IVF stuff at the moment and one of them is up to about nine or 10 attempts, and the financial burden on top of the stress is just massive. I'd love to be able to help people out with things like that.

Oh my gosh, I love this. You have such clarity around your goals. Tell us more about your investments in shares and farming.

I've currently got about $70,000 in shares. We pulled a lot of money out of that to build the house and then we pulled more out to buy the farm as well. I started saving as a teenager because of the drought. Any birthday money I got, or if I did some wool classing, I'd save whatever I earnt. When I turned 18, I had about $10,000 because all I'd done was save; I didn't spend a thing.

With that, I went and caught up with one of my friends who's a financial advisor. He offered to teach me about the stock market for free. That's where it started from. And from there, we've now got two farms.

So what do the financials look like on those properties?

There's no debt on the first farm at the moment. On the second farm we've got about $550,000 of debt.

One of the farms is worth about $1.4 million and the other's worth about $1.25 million. It's been a lot of hard work and it's taken time for it to grow in value. So it's not just capital we put in; it's grown over time.

All of that and you've just turned 30! You grew up in farming but how did you get this work–life balance and this motivation to do all these additional things? From your family?

No, definitely not. My dad and my grandparents thought you should just work on the farm, you don't have time for anything else. It's long hours. But because of the drought, I really wanted to be able to help out financially if things got bad again. So that's where my savings came into play. I thought if I could build up some spare income, I might be able to bail the farm out if we got into trouble. I was really scared that we'd lose the place. I didn't want that to happen because that's where I grew up, my parents grew up, my grandpa grew up. It's a big thing for our family. Financially backing that if I ever had to was always my goal.

So it was always in the back of my mind to make money elsewhere. It's really important to have that work–life balance but it's really tricky not to get burnt out. And that's something I've focused on because I used to get burnt out a lot. When I met my husband he sat me down one day and told me I just needed to stop and to make sure I was looking after myself. You can't get burnt out every week. You work really hard and you get a lot done, but then you're out for four days because you're bedridden or in hospital or whatever. So it's been a steep learning curve.

He sounds like a good egg, your partner. Does he make you tea and toast on the weekends?

He does, yeah.

Tell us a bit more about your debt: is there any other debt sitting around that you haven't shared?

No, just that $550,000 on the second farm, but with the house build it'll probably grow to around $1 million. Houses are expensive. And they've really gone up in the last 12 months. Our initial quote has blown out even more so we've put away some cash ready for that.

She's *on the* Money

The costs of housing and of raising children are likely to be your two biggest lifetime expenses. For many embarking on these journeys for the first time, the focus is on reaching the first hurdle; saving enough for a deposit, or covering the cost of pregnancy. For those undertaking surrogacy or IVF these costs can be substantial.

So it's somewhat understandable when setting out towards these exciting milestones that less attention is given to the longer-term costs. But, my friends, these are just as, if not more, important! Mortgages are generally set over thirty years and parenting officially lasts until your child is 18 (and then some!).

It's really important to make sure you've sat down and worked out the lifetime costs of these commitments and made plans for covering them in the event of various scenarios, including illness or injury. Insurances are something worth investigating; not just for your material possessions, but to cover you, personally. That way, if your income is affected, you'll still be able to keep a roof over your head and your family fed.

A million dollars is a lot of money, do you think this is your forever family home?

We're building it on my partner's family farm, and you can't really just sell a house on a farm, so it is a forever kind of thing. That's why we're spending the money now. We've done the hard yards to get to this point and we've ticked all the boxes. We've budgeted and our stars have aligned to have this baby and we want to have a nice house to bring our baby home to. We're making sure we spend the money where it's needed.

Who else lives on the family farm?

There are a couple of other houses. My partner's parents live in the main farmhouse and then one of his sisters lives in the other one. There are six kids in his family and some live in the local town and nearby, so everyone's still pretty close by. My husband and I are living in a little cottage and we don't have to pay rent or anything.

That's a money win.

Yeah, it is. We just have to pay the electricity and that's about it.

How often do you get to do big family dinners?

At least once a week. Sometimes we'll have a little catch-up at lunchtimes too; it's such a buzz with six kids and all those grand-kids. And they're going to get another one soon!

I want to ask about childcare. You said earlier that you and your partner essentially earn the same amount. What's the plan when you have a newborn?

There's been a lot of discussion about that lately and a lot to think about. There's a childcare centre in town which is 10 minutes away, but it's hard to get into because it's a small town and the centre can only handle a certain number of kids. As soon as we know that we're pregnant, we have to put our name on the list. So we'll do that and whatever days we get, we'll take. We're lucky that we have my partner's parents and they're happy to help out. And when I'm doing the financials, like the budgets, hopefully I can look after the baby at the same time.

What do you think is your best money habit?

Probably our best habit is living below our means. We've never really been big spenders. Communication's really important in our relationship and we're very clear about our goals. We talk about money all the time. Whenever we have a bath, we talk about money!

And what about your worst money habit?

Our worst is probably the bakery. I always end up at the bakery!

What are we buying at the bakery?

Like a little veggie pie. They're amazing. Or a spinach sausage roll. We're always doing filming jobs, so we're on the road a lot going to other farms and we happen to drive past the bakery all the time, so we just pop in . . .

Do you think that your money grade is still an A? What do you think it would take to get from an A to an A plus?

I think it's still an A. It's been a long journey and no-one should compare themselves to each other. So I'm happy with that. To get to an A plus, I probably need all those goals ticked off and for us to be helping people as much as possible. Once we get there, then we can put that plus sign on.

WORK JOURNALLING PROMPTS

What do you love to do – is there a way you might make some extra money from doing it on the side?

What do you hate to do – might you be better off paying someone else to do it, to free you up to focus on the things you're good at?

What's the hardest conversation around work, time and money that you need to have? Journal some thoughtful questions that will help the conversation get started.

Do you know what you're worth in your industry? When was the last time you reviewed current salaries for similar roles? What extra skills could you acquire to make you stand out and attract a higher earning capacity?

Work Money Wins

ANNALIESE started a new job that is fully work-from-home and noticed a huge difference in her spending. She is saving money on fuel and also has more time and energy to cook at home, so she doesn't have to rely on takeaway meals anymore either.

ELLIE'S dream job was advertised a few weeks prior to when she was due to return to her old position from maternity leave. She wasn't going to apply, but she had VD in her ear reminding her that men apply for jobs without the perfect level of experience all the time and women should do the same – so she went for it. She was offered a contract position with a plan to work towards a permanent position! She gets a pay rise, better flexibility and it will look great on her CV. Congrats Ellie!

DANA was inspired by VD's words and asked her boss for a pay rise based on the increased cost of living. Her boss praised her for presenting well and was pleased that she had met with him about it. She ended up with the pay rise, all because she asked!

JEAN quit a new job after eight weeks when she found it to be toxic – it had sounded great on paper but in reality, the company failed her own probation tests and didn't fit with her values. For Jean, the big money win in this is saving the future costs associated with the stress and health impacts from the job if she'd decided to stay.

VENRINDER decided to apply for a scholarship for educational learning from her workplace, not sure of her chances of getting it. She was offered $1000 to upskill and become an international board certified lactation consultant!

TIINA has a cleaning business and had some cancellations, and spotted an advertisement for someone looking for a cleaner. She easily made up the $300 she would have lost and was given, to keep, extra cleaning products worth hundreds of dollars! On top of that, Tiina's new client sold her some expensive plant pots for well under the retail price – a reminder that lovely and generous people do exist.

HANNAH recently got a salary increase with some well-presented written justifications of her achievements in her role. To make the most of the extra income, she readjusted her budget and transactions, putting the extra money directly towards debt repayments and levelling up her emergency fund, before it could be swallowed up by lifestyle creep.

CAT started a fairy floss and popcorn side gig back in 2019, pivoting it to a delivery business when COVID hit. Her business ended up booming!

Debt

When used wisely, debt can be a great tool. But if we're not fully aware of how it works, it can pretty quickly become a slippery downhill slope leading to a debt-shame cycle that's hard to escape. With debt so readily available, from buy now, pay later schemes to credit cards and personal loans, and given how little financial training we receive, it's no wonder many of us get caught out.

My purpose with She's on the Money is to provide the inspiration and education to help people move from victim to hero of their own financial success story. Understanding your mindset around scarcity, borrowing and the difference between 'good' and 'bad' debt is a great place to start. These stories from the community reveal all that and more, showing that no matter where you begin, your future is bright!

A Decade in Debt to Her Dream Job

This money diarist grew up with a single mum who had *nine* credit cards! After leaving home at 16 with nothing but the clothes on her back, then spending the next decade in debt, she has finally now, aged 30, managed to land her dream job, double her income, get debt-free and start saving for her first home. How did she do it?

What grade would you give your money habits, from A to F?

At the moment, probably a B plus.

Can you tell us a little more about your money story?

I had quite a troubled upbringing. I was raised by a single mother and although she provided for us financially, emotionally and support-wise, we struggled. We didn't have a great connection and I didn't receive a lot of mentorship around how to handle finances. We never went without; we had passes to theme parks and went on holidays, but it was all funded through debt. At the time I thought it was normal because she was working and raising two kids on her own, but it did have an impact on my money story. I wanted to start working as soon as possible because I understood that to get the things you want in life, you need your own income.

As soon as I turned 14 and was able to work, I got a job. Unfortunately, I didn't have access to my money, so I had no appreciation for how to save. My mum held my key card so she controlled my spending, and I think that was to my detriment. If I'd been able to manage my own finances, I would have had a better understanding of how to budget and might have avoided seeking instant gratification.

Do you think that came from her trying to protect you from running out of money or was it more of a control thing?

Definitely a control thing. *Everything* had to be under her control, but I was quite independent from a young age, so that was a sore spot. Not long after I started working, our relationship really went downhill, which led to me being kicked out of home.

What was your first job?

I worked in retail on the checkout, both days of the weekend and on night shifts when I could, though obviously school played a massive factor in how many hours I could get. I was working for a whole $8 an hour, which felt rich back in the day!

Frustrating that you couldn't access it. Did that lead to arguments or resentment?

Not necessarily. I've always been, I wouldn't say materialistic, but I like nice things. I'm very proud of my home. Even back then, at age 15, I wanted to buy a rug, so I bought myself a $600 rug. I also funded a trip to the snow through school. So I *was* able to buy things with that money, but it would have been more beneficial to my future self if I'd been able to learn a bit more about how to better manage my finances. I mean, I probably would have spent more on silly things too, if I'd had unrestricted access, so I may not have been able to buy those nice things, but I would have learnt more and built a better foundation.

From having things taken off you and your spending controlled, you've now created financial freedom. Tell us about the pivot point.

Between 18 and 28, I was stuck in a revolving door of getting myself in and then out of debt. I was living on my own and earning a decent income for my age, but always lived beyond my means. I earnt enough to cover groceries and lead a decent lifestyle, but then I'd want to shout my friends drinks or go shopping. So I said to myself, you know what you need? You need a safety net – go get yourself a $500 credit card. And that was the start of the spiral. I got myself a credit card and it just went downhill from there.

I was constantly refinancing and getting credit cards re-balanced, just to avoid interest. I don't know how I knew that interest was bad, but that was where I drew the line. I told myself it was okay to be in debt, as long as I kept paying it down. And I did. I could always afford my repayments and never defaulted on anything, but in that 10-year period I had at least five personal loans and about 10 credit cards. I was paying them down, getting balance transfers and doing everything to avoid additional fees, but I just constantly lived beyond my means.

She's *on the* Money

When I got out of uni, I ended up with $40,000 worth of personal debt, which all started in exactly the same way – with a $500 credit card. It was a card that earnt points, so it felt like a money saving *and* money savvy. But then, it spiralled out of control because that piece of plastic gave me access to a lifestyle I hadn't had before.

Carrying debt can be fine, so long as you're not racking up a whole heap of interest. In fact, it can be smart if you're using it to get ahead – for things like education or growth investments. But for most of us coming out of school, we just aren't that money wise.

Financial literacy, especially as young teens with our first jobs, does us a bit of a dirty, because you just don't know what you don't know. I knew interest was bad – I didn't want to pay money for owing money – but I was happy to pay back the money I owed. That didn't feel too bad.

What I hadn't learnt was how quickly debt can compound. So you might start borrowing more to pay back the debt you owe, but then you owe money on that debt, and soon it gets out of control. The buy now, pay later schemes can be especially bad for that.

Before you take on any debt it's super important to know what you're getting yourself into and to have a solid plan for repaying your loan within the repayment window, or you may just end up very quickly owing more and more money.

A hard thing for me is that my close friends have had a lot of financial support from their parents. So, although I never felt like I was going without because I financed my lifestyle myself, I did feel bad that I didn't have the things that they had. I had to remind myself that I was doing it on my own and that's okay. It took me a long time to come to terms with the fact that you're never going to travel at the same pace as everyone else. You just have to stick to your own lane and educate yourself. I'm a massive advocate now for educating yourself on financial literacy. It's such a shame that it's not taught in schools, not even the basic fundamentals of tax and super.

So you've changed gears and you now have your dream job. What do you do and how much money do you earn?

I'm an analyst in the energy industry. I started late last year and it's my dream job. With bonuses, I'm on just over $130,000 plus super.

Are you kidding? That's incredible!

I know – I'm still pinching myself! When I was 27, I was earning $60,000 and had reached the point where I knew I'd outgrown my workplace. I'd just finished uni and the boss was like, oh, I understand you've just finished uni, but I don't think it's suitable to give you a raise at this point. Essentially saying he didn't think I was worth the money. But, given that I was managing his business and a team of six people, I felt otherwise. I knew it was time to move on.

I had a dream company in mind – I'd always been really appreciative of their staff and customer service – so I reached out to a recruiter and managed to land a job there. In the two years I've been working there, I've had two promotions. When the opportunity came up to become an analyst, I knew I had to step up from my first role or I'd regret it. Everything's just fallen into place.

I think I'm getting ahead because of my attitude – I wanted the job and I'm passionate about it, and I guess that just sort of flows through. I've always had a strong work ethic, it's probably one of the things I'm most proud of. I find it difficult to see good qualities in myself, but my work ethic is something that's never faltered.

I can tell that means a lot to you – even more than just the money.

Last year when I accepted the original role, I ended up regretting it. I'd chosen the role for financial reasons – it was a $25,000 increase and I was like, how can I pass this up? I knew I would do well in the role, so I took it, but after a few months, I realised it wasn't the right fit as it really deviated from my values. So I've learnt my lesson there. My new role is challenging me – in a great way. The team are incredible and I'm getting an awesome paycheque to go with it.

Let's talk about your money goals. What are you working towards?

I'm currently saving for a house, but I only have $11,000 saved. I'd listened to the *Barefoot Investor* and then I started looking at other ways to get more financially literate. I found *She's on the Money* and have listened to every single episode! It helps keep me on track and accountable if I'm ever second guessing myself.

When I began this journey, I had money in savings, but still had a credit card debt. A chunk of interest came through and I realised I had enough money in my savings to pay off the credit card debt and stop getting charged interest. So I paid it off and it was honestly the best feeling in the world.

I've had about 18 months now of being debt free and I'm saving about 35 per cent of my salary. I've been able to save for a trip, for my thirtieth birthday, to Europe for a few weeks. And now, I'm focusing on saving to buy a house.

What would 25-year-old you think about your situation today?

She would probably say, I knew you'd get there eventually! From a young age, I always wanted to own my own house. It's security for me – something that's mine that no-one can take away. I always knew that by the time I was 30, I wanted to achieve that. It might not happen right on 30, but I am going to get there.

Fantastic. So you're basically out of debt and have been debt free for 18 months now. Are you investing?

Yes, I am. I have about $5000 invested in CommSec.

How have you chosen your investments?

I'm focusing on diversification. I have a couple of high-risk lithium stocks that I keep just for growth, but I focus primarily on ETFs to provide me with diversification, lower risk and paid dividends. With the income I receive, I reinvest that and let it grow – I don't touch it and I don't overthink it.

I do have a HECS debt of about $33,000. At nearly 7 per cent this year, I'm not looking forward to indexation in June!

Yeah, that makes me feel physically ill. What are your thoughts on that?

If the indexation is 7 per cent, I'm not going to worry about paying it off. I'd rather have that money sit there in my bank account ready for my home loan. Unfortunately, having a HECS debt does wipe about $100,000 off my borrowing capacity, so I did think about taking care of it, but I decided it's just going to sit there in the background. I feel it's better than having an interest-earning loan and I'm okay with it – that education debt is what's enabled me to earn the income I'm on.

From having 10 credit cards and personal loans, to now being in the financially responsible position you're in, what would you say to people experiencing a similar situation?

Take baby steps. Assess your situation. There are so many different ways to knock down your debt, but do things that are going to help you hit your milestones sooner, so you can get that amazing debt-free feeling. Nothing beats it when you pay off a credit card and you shut it down. My buy now, pay later loans were the first debts I got rid of and after that I paid down the credit card. Obviously the increases in my income were a massive help too. I made sure that when I got paid extra, I didn't spend it, but used it to pay down my debt.

What do you think your best money habit is?

I've always been good at budgeting. Even when I was in debt, I always calculated my monthly expenses and put a set amount away each week to cover them.

What kind of budgeting are you doing now?

If I take money out of my savings, I feel guilty now. I value lunches and dinners out, which is probably my worst money habit. But knowing what my monthly and annual costs are, I put that into my bill hub. And then I've got my savings goals, so everything's accounted for.

I get paid monthly though and it kills me! No matter how much I try and budget, I'm always taking money out of my savings and then having to replenish it the next month. There's always a little bit of a buffer, and I make sure that I keep myself accountable. So though I do run a strict budget, I constantly review it, to make sure I'm okay with everything.

It's basically a matter of acknowledging that sometimes things aren't in your control. You can overanalyse, which I think makes you feel guilty, because you feel like you're not doing enough. If I've overspent for the month, I try not to punish myself, but I do feel guilty that I've not met the budget I set for myself, so perhaps I need to review my strategy.

She's *on the* Money

When it comes to budgeting, there's a lot to consider. I think people tend to forget all the 'extra' things that pop up. They should all be taken into consideration in the budget: your friend's birthday, your mum's birthday, health check-ups, good and bad 'surprises'. It's not that we 'go over' budget, it's just that we didn't plan efficiently the first time.

Well, I feel like you've come so far. You have this epic salary. You're already well on the way to saving for your first home. You're putting away 35 per cent of your salary. You're about to celebrate 30. You have a $5000 investment portfolio. You've got your emergency fund. And you've got a strategy for your HECS. Would you still give your money habits a B plus?

Maybe an A minus. There's always room for improvement!

Like a Phoenix Rising From the Ashes

Content warning: this story contains details of an abusive relationship.

Fourteen years ago, this money diarist was in a mentally, emotionally, physically, sexually and financially abusive relationship. Once she left, she still had to disentangle herself from the web of deceit her ex had trapped her in, not least, a staggering $120,000 in credit card debts that continued to accrue interest. Finally, at age 46, after seven long years and having paid back almost $250,000, she's met the love of her life, owns her own property and is finally free – a true phoenix rising from the ashes.

Let's start at the start. Can you tell us a bit about your money story?

I grew up in a single-parent family where money was always

tight. We're talking homebrand food and homemade clothes. I never went hungry – there was always a roof over my head and food in the pantry – we just didn't have much more than the basics. Once I left home, I knew I didn't want that for myself. But because of life circumstances growing up, I made a bunch of silly decisions and ended up getting involved with someone who was the worst person I could have ever gotten involved with. I ended up in a very deep hole financially, but decided that I didn't want to go bankrupt. So I fought my way back, paid it all off, and I'm so happy that my life is so much different now.

I'm really proud of you. Can you tell us what your attitude towards money is now?

As I say, growing up, money was tight, and there's absolutely nothing wrong with homebrand stuff. I still buy that every day, but it can become kind of a stigma in your life. I've got my head screwed on straight, finally. Now I see money, not as the scarce resource I used to think it was, but as a means to enjoy myself – the reward I get for putting in so much hard work. I have a day job and a couple of side hustles. I put in a lot of hours, so the money's the reward for that. When I go out, I like to splurge every now and then. And I don't think that's a bad thing, because I'm not robbing from Peter to pay Paul. I budget for it.

Oh, my gosh, I love this. So tell us about your main job and your side hustles.

I am so excited to answer this question because I've changed things so much in the last six months. I got a job as an analyst at a new company last year and my numbers are so much better than before. I'm currently on a salary of $95,000 and get 13 per cent super on top of that. We also have an annual bonus scheme which maxes out at 10 per cent.

Money win! And the side hustles? How much money do you earn from those? And how much time does it take you each week?

I have three side hustles. A craft business where I create things with my hands – it lets me get my artistic streak out, which is very different to my logical and spreadsheet-based day job.

My second side hustle is a wholesale supply store for the kind of crafts that I do – I sell to other people like me, other makers. That turns over about $200,000 a year. It's not enough to live on, because the actual profit after I've taken everything out is only about half of my annual salary, so I'm not ready to give up my day job yet, but I know that I can grow the store further. I don't want it to get too big too quick. I know that managing growth is a delicate balance.

Thirdly, I'm also in the process of setting up a clothing and homewares brand, but I'm finding it really hard to find the extra time to dedicate to getting it off the ground. So that's just in its infancy at the moment.

Wow, they sound more like full-time jobs than side hustles. Amazing! And what is your big money goal?

All the money that was previously going towards my credit card repayments is being saved for a massive relocation that we're hoping to do next year. My partner and I want a bit of a tree change and we want to find our dream home in a quieter area. Ultimately, I want to retire in the next 10 to 15 years.

With that type of income, you definitely can achieve that. It's exciting.

It really is. And we deserve it. I keep pinching myself and going, is this real?! And my other half just tells me that it is, that I deserve it – that *we* deserve it.

You do. It sounds like you've worked really hard to get there. Do you currently invest?

I certainly do. I've got $170,000 in my super. It's not very much, but 10 years ago I only had $12,000, so I've put aside a fair whack. My balance was well below the average when I first looked at it, so I worked hard to get it back up. I'm probably a bit above people in my age bracket now, so that's good.

I've also got two portfolios worth about $2500 with Spaceship and I do my round-ups through Raiz. I've got about $4500 there and I love Raiz because I've never noticed a single cent of that money leaving my account.

Round-ups are so powerful because they're incidental, small things, but they really add up. You've got $4500 saved and you're saying you didn't even feel it?

I never noticed it going out of my account! I also do micro investing. That's like my play money, total gambles – I don't care if I lose it. I've only put in $175, but I've gotten some huge returns on my picks there, so I've got about $500 in those at the moment.

And finally, I also have about $2500 in ETFs via the Selfwealth app. That's where I'm funnelling all of my savings at the moment.

You're very diversified. I want to flip this and ask about debts now, because I know you paid off a pretty big debt. Do you currently have any other debt?

The only debt that I have is the mortgage and I'm so proud of that. My consumer debt is all gone!

Making my final payment felt amazing. I was doing some sums one day and realised I had enough to get rid of the last little bit on my final card. So I made some phone calls and sent the last payment. I work from home, so I raced next door and said to my neighbour, oh, my gosh, I've just done it! I've finally made the last payment!

Then I drove down the road to the BWS and bought myself a really expensive bottle of champagne. It was the best glass of champagne I've had in my life!

She's *on the* Money

So many times when we're in these situations, it stretches out. Paying off the debt seems to take forever. And then, finally one day, you click the 'transfer' button and it feels really incidental. One side of you is like, yahoo, that part of my life is done! But, at the same time, it's not very exciting. You just click the button and it's over.

But we *do* need to celebrate these moments! It's so important to take the opportunity to run next door, to get some champagne, and to actually enjoy it. To honour the occasion! We need to embrace these milestones. You don't want to just sit there and be all, oh, we're done, and then . . . nothing.

Congratulations, that is so well deserved! Do you have any savvy spending or saving hacks, like reward schemes for online shopping?

I don't, because I don't actually shop online. I've moved over to a cash system – I'm a cash envelope stuffer! My wallet comes with me whenever I want to spend money. I can't spend when I don't have cash.

Oh my gosh, that's genius. It makes so much sense, especially if you're a visual learner.

I find it really helps to picture how much I'm going to have left. Let's say it's pay day and I've got $100 worth of spending money in my purse. If I want to go and get sushi, and that'll cost me $30, then it means taking a third of my money out of my purse. If I'm just tapping plastic, I don't notice it.

Then, for online stuff, like investing, once the cash I'm saving hits $1000, I go and deposit it in the bank and after that, I can move it around online.

Epic. I love that. I want to know what your best money habit is.

I'm an analyst by trade, so huge on spreadsheets and data. I have this massive spreadsheet that has every single bill I've ever paid and all of the estimated amounts and dates going forward for the next 12 months. It includes our household budget and shows how much needs to be transferred into each of our little sub-accounts when we get paid. Back when I was paying off my debt, it showed all of my repayment projections, so I could see when each card was due to get paid off. I use it to calculate my net worth every month.

And what about your worst money habit?

I think my worst money habit is probably that I like a bit of luxury in my life. I am very fond of the finer things, probably because I struggled for so long. Now that I'm not on struggle street anymore, I prefer to fly business and I really love saving up all my points so that occasionally I can upgrade to first class. I like splurging on expensive hotels. And I don't just get the basic room – I get the club room on the highest floor with the cocktail bar and the free nibbles!

That's not a bad money habit; that is you living your best life because you absolutely deserve it. Looking at everything in balance, what grade would you give your money habits?

I'm gonna put tickets on myself here. I think I deserve an A.

You do. You absolutely do. For anyone else who may be struggling, can you tell us a bit about the situation you found yourself in?

About 14 years ago, I got involved with a man who very quickly became my abuser, and it was just the worst time of my life. Towards the end, he was showing the scariest of all of the abuse types. I knew that if I stayed much longer, I wouldn't make it out alive. So 10 years ago, I finally went and got some psychological help for the first time in my life. My psychologist helped me find the strength within to leave. They say that it takes a survivor, on average, about seven attempts to get out. I managed to do it on my sixth attempt, which I'm really proud of.

Once I got out, I reconnected with all my friends and my family whom my abuser had cut me off from. I could use the bathroom without permission. I could go grocery shopping. I could do anything I wanted! And I didn't have someone yelling at me all the time. It was like I had this whole new life. I'd escaped and I was free.

But then, a couple of months later, the nightmare returned – but in a different way. These credit card statements started showing up, which I had no idea about. It turned out he'd taken out cards in my name. I thought I had two credit cards with a $2000 limit. But when I finally got to see my bank statements, he'd increased those credit limits and had also applied for all these other ones in my name. He'd stolen my driver's licence and forged my signature and then he'd maxed everything out.

It took a heap of digging to get to the bottom of it – I had to go and get credit reports in order to find some of the cards, because he'd put different addresses on them and the post wasn't even coming to the house. I tallied it all up and it was $126,000 that I owed, and I was just petrified. I was so scared. I had no idea how on earth I was going to get out of it. And we're talking 10 years ago, well before the banking reform and before banks had domestic violence and hardship policies in place, so I was on the hook for all of it.

I went to the police and they spoke to him, but he said that I knew about the cards and that I'd signed all the forms. So it was my word against his and I had no proof. It was awful. I briefly considered going bankrupt, but I knew that I wanted to buy a house one day and I knew that I wanted to keep my options open for a possible career change in the future, and I knew that if you've been bankrupt, you can't get some jobs. So I decided that bankruptcy wasn't something I personally wanted to go through.

The first thing I did was to move everything I could across to 0 per cent interest cards. Then I called all of the banks and asked them to close the accounts and just let me pay them off slowly so that nothing else could possibly get added to them. It took me almost seven years and the total payback figure was $247,414.84.

She's *on the* Money

It can be like having blinkers on when you have that much debt staring you in the face, especially coming out of a domestic violence situation. Understandably, many people turn immediately to bankruptcy as a solution, thinking, oh, that'll get me out of the situation, okay, let's just do that. And they don't tend to think through the ramifications that it might bring later down the track.

Bankruptcy isn't for everybody. If you want to work in certain industries or in certain roles, or you want to buy a house within a certain period of time, bankruptcy could potentially put the brakes on those dreams.

Like I always say, before making any significant financial decision, it is so, so, so important to get *all* the information and spend some time absorbing it and understanding it – all the details and the fine print. Then think through your values and what's really important to you – both current you and future you. From there, you'll be empowered to make the decision that's right for you and your personal circumstances. Everyone is different.

So, what's next? Where do you see yourself going?

Along the way, while I was paying down the debt, I also bought a block of land, saved up a deposit and built a house. I bought the cheapest block of land in a housing estate a long way away from where I wanted to actually live. I built this miniscule house on it. It was just big enough for me and my dogs. That was all that I needed at the time. I had a second job to help with saving up the deposit, but then . . .

I met a wonderful, patient, kind, understanding human. I got engaged and then got married. We had these two amazing overseas trips. But we did all of that in a really scaled-down way. When we got married, we had a micro wedding. There were only 20 people there, and it was a bit of a surprise. We only told the people who were going to be invited. After the ceremony, we jumped on a public bus and went to a restaurant down the road and had our wedding reception there. It was all we needed and wanted. We had the people who mattered the most with us there on the day, and we didn't get into any debt. I think it only cost us about $5000.

So now, we're hoping to relocate towards the end of next year. We're aggressively paying down our current mortgage at the moment.

Love it. How did you know that you could buy a block of land and build a house and do all of these things while you were paying off that massive debt? What resources did you rely on?

To get myself free of the whole situation, I got a lot of help from a domestic violence support group in the city close to where I live. They were really helpful with information about what grants were available and which lenders could help you get back on your feet. I knew I needed to get out of the situation I was in, so it was head down, bum up, get it done. I just put every spare second of my time towards achieving the goal of being safe in my own housing. And I did it.

What made you decide to pay the debt, rather than pursue legal action?

I know it was a lot of money, but I also knew I'd prefer to pay it than to have *any* conversation about this person ever again.

When you have a domestic violence situation, you have to go back for another hearing to have it extended. I knew I couldn't show up to that, because I'd be in the same room as him. It was a case of, I just need to put this behind me. And I knew that the kindest way to do that, for my soul, was to get it done myself.

What steps did you take following on from that? Were there any things you did to make sure that something like that couldn't happen again?

There's a legal service specifically for women who have escaped from domestic violence. They assisted me by drafting a letter that I sent to about 30 or 40 financial institutions guaranteeing that I would never be applying for credit. Basically I told them not to accept anything with my details on it. And nothing has ever come up. I check regularly, and I think I'm in the clear now.

You found out about a lot of these debts because you looked at your credit score. Do you wish you'd known to check that sooner?

I'm in two minds. I've delved into a lot of stuff from that time with my shrink and part of me thinks that credit reports should be sent to every person as soon as they turn 18. But there's another part of me that thinks, well, if I had known back then, before I was ready to escape, I would have just accepted what he was telling me, and I wouldn't have been able to fight back. And then it might have been even worse.

It's interesting how you might think it was a really shitty situation, but in hindsight, the cards fell in exactly the way they were meant to. Now you're in this beautiful position

that you absolutely deserve to be in, what would you say to yourself from 14 years ago?

I think I would tell her, you can survive anything! You have the drive and the passion and the will inside of you. But more importantly, you have the strength.

And you know, *everybody* has. You just need to figure out how to harness it. I firmly believe that if anyone is in a similar situation and they don't know how to get out, they should go and speak to their GP. Go and get a mental healthcare plan and then go and get some psychotherapy sessions which are free if your practitioner bulk bills. They will help you to find that strength and power within. They will help you get out safely, because without knowing how to escape a relationship like that safely, it can actually be really dangerous.

Thanks to my shrink, we got a whole heap of stuff lined up and got all my ducks in a row before I made a move. It made the break so much easier, because I had someone there to help me take control and say, these are the steps we're going to follow. Before that, I had absolutely no idea what steps I needed to take.

When I was still in the relationship, I didn't have a card for my own bank account. He had it, so I didn't have access to money. He would top up my train ticket. He would do the grocery shopping. If I hadn't been able to go to a bulk-billing GP and get referred to a subsidised psychologist, I don't think I would have been able to get out. So make sure you articulate your situation and specific needs to your GP, so they can help get you the support you need. And always ask your medical practitioners if they'll bulk bill.

Another great resource is the National Debt Helpline. They have lots of good free resources and free financial counsellors. Never be afraid to say you need help because we all do sometimes. You're not alone, and I hope I've been a little bit of a voice of inspiration for someone who needs it.

Jail, Debt and Learning to Be Free

This money diarist has had a crazy ride on life's financial rollercoaster. She grew up in a wealthy household, but when she was 15, her dad was sent to prison for drug manufacturing – their house was raided and their assets seized, the whole nine yards. From this moment on, she was determined to be self-sustaining and after this rocky start, now aged 31, she's totally turned the ship around.

First things first, what grade would you give your money habits?

I would give myself a B plus.

That's pretty good. Tell us a bit more about your money story.

I was very spoilt growing up and pretty much got everything I wanted. We'd go on holidays all the time, that sort of thing. But when I was a teenager, I was woken up one morning by a police officer telling me I had to go sit in our living room while our house was being raided. It was horrific. My dad was convicted of drug manufacturing and for the next 14 years he was behind bars. This was shocking, obviously, and really confronting. It was probably the worst for my mum, because she had no idea what had been going on or where the money had been coming from.

Everything we had was taken away; not only material assets, but the lifestyle of holidays and buying whatever we wanted. It was a total shock. We had to learn how to navigate life without money. It was hard, because my mum hadn't worked for about 10 years – she'd stopped when my youngest sibling was born.

Oh my gosh, what's it like having your house raided?

It's not nice. If I had to sum it up in one word, it would be 'terrifying'. Even now I find thinking about it scary. We were all treated like criminals, even though we were just little kids and had no idea what was going on . . . They went through all our personal stuff, made a whole lot of mess, and then just left us to clean it up. Whatever they took, they took; we never saw it again. They seized cars, houses, the lot.

That is literally the worst. And obviously you had no idea about what was going on.

Absolutely no idea. I mean, some people's side hustle is cleaning cars or walking dogs. Apparently, my dad's was manufacturing drugs.

So what happened with your mum, because that would have been heartbreaking for her. She loses her husband then has to learn how to budget and cash flow and deal with you and your siblings on her own.

Yeah, it was a huge shock for her, very confronting, and it took a long time for her to find her feet. Imagine having your lifelong partner just taken away from you, the person you've always relied on. At first, she was kind of stick-your-head-in-the-sand and do whatever is the next best thing. Any money we had went towards solicitor bills.

Then, eventually, it got to the point where the mortgage wasn't being paid and everything was in arrears. When I was in my early twenties, I was asked to have our mortgage transferred to me. It was sold to me as a good thing, so I did it to save the family home. It was the worst decision I ever made.

Gosh, that doesn't sound good. Why so bad?

Well, my mum and dad technically still own the house, but their debt is in my name . . . so I can't really move forward unless it gets sold. I can't get a first home buyer grant and now that I'm married, my husband and I can't get the grant together, either. He could apply for it by himself, but then I'd always be behind, because I don't own it.

What is the benefit to your parents in having their debt in your name? Was it because they legally couldn't have a mortgage anymore?

Because the mortgage wasn't getting paid, the house was going to be repossessed. By transferring it to me, we could keep it in the family. I mean, it's just bricks and mortar, so why not just get rid of it, right? But I guess it's that generation – wanting to hold onto the things that they put their blood, sweat and tears into. So, that's the benefit. It's still in the family, and eventually, they want to be able to buy it back. But their credit history isn't the best, plus they obviously have to prove servicing and all that kind of stuff, so I'm not sure how that's ever going to happen.

So are your mum and dad still together after all of this?

Yeah.

What a journey for them to go through. But where does that leave you – what do you currently do for work? How much money do you earn?

Currently, I'm in business development and I also have an online coaching business, as a personal trainer, on the side. In my full-time role, I earn $110,000 excluding super. And in my side hustle, I make between $10,000 to $30,000 a year, depending how much time and effort I put into it.

Very cool. How did you start your side hustle and how do you promote it?

I was always a personal trainer, then after doing a whole bunch of extra courses, I decided to move my coaching online. I just think it delivers so much more value. Other than the time factor, you get so much more bang for your buck if you have an online coach rather than an in-person coach. In person, you pay $100 and see them for 45 minutes and they just run you through a workout. As an online coach, I give my clients a full program with all of their exercises and nutrition guidelines – and it's always available. I also do weekly video check-ins where I monitor their progress and what's going on with their body.

Queen! What about your big money goal – what are you working towards?

Our big money goal was actually our wedding which we managed to pay for in cash!

Congratulations! Tell us more. When did you get married? How did you budget for it?

We got married late last year. It was amazing, but as you know, when it comes to wedding budgets, initially you think it's going to be one thing and then you get into it and it's a whole different ball game! It's the shock of your lifetime!

I mean, I knew weddings were expensive, so I knew that spending $20,000 would be unrealistic – unless you're having a backyard party or something really small – but I'd never wanted that and neither did my husband. So we went into it thinking we'd probably have to spend around $40,000 to $45,000. We decided we'd choose the top things that we wanted to spend money on, like photography, videography, food, entertainment and the venue. I was in full budget mode, but there are so many other things that just add up. Very quickly we realised $45,000 wasn't going to cut it. Then we realised $65,000 wasn't going to cut it. It ended up being around $80,000, but it was perfect. I wouldn't change a thing.

Sounds amazing. In terms of pricing, what was the thing that most shocked you?

The flowers! It was wild. I still can't believe that flowers can possibly cost so much. We had a budget for them, but then they said, double it – no actually, triple it! And then because of all the floods last year, they went up even more, because it was harder to get them. And I don't do things small.

She's on the Money

Before you start planning a wedding you think you'll be really conscious about the spending. And goodness knows, you try! But even if you have a great partner who says not to cut anything because you'll regret it, you still feel bad and you still can't quite believe how much it's all costing!

The most important thing is to have the conversation – before, during and after – to get, and to keep, your values aligned. Determine the negotiables and non-negotiables for each of you and find ways to compromise so that you both get what you want. I mean, it's so, so, so important to agree on what things you're willing to fight for and what you're willing to let go. Not just for your wedding, but for the ongoing happiness of your relationship. Like all important things, it will take effort and conversation and compromise. But I know that *you* know, it's worth it.

It's so surprising how involved your partner gets. Even though I thought I'd be planning everything, it wasn't the case. I'm usually the doer and he just follows. Initially, he complained that he had to write a speech because he thought he just had to show up! And I was like, no, sir. But the more we went along, the more he got into it. He did a great job!

And now you're off on your honeymoon which is happening a bit of a way past your wedding. How did you decide on the timing?

Because our wedding was so expensive, we needed time to save for the honeymoon – we hadn't included it in our wedding budget. We've saved like crazy since the wedding as the honeymoon is going to be a bit longer than the usual and travel costs have doubled. But I'm happy that, in both cases, we've saved the money before spending it. And I never regret spending money on experiences.

And when you get back from your honeymoon, what's your money goal?

We're going to knuckle down and save for a deposit to buy a house.

That's exciting and so fun, all these big-ticket items being ticked off. So, alongside all this saving and spending, do you have any investments?

I have my super, which is about $55,000. I was a bit shocked when I checked – I swear last time I looked it was much lower than that. And then we have about $8000 in ETFs and shares, and then a few thousand in crypto, which I just kind of leave alone.

And what about debts?

I currently have $1500 left on a loan that started out at over $30,000 from consolidating all my credit card debt. It's only about 8 per cent interest and I'll be paying it off as soon as we get back from our honeymoon.

What are you going to do when you pay it off? I feel like it's always super anticlimactic.

We have a plan to maybe go out for a dinner, or open a bottle of champagne. There has to be something, because when you submit your final debt repayment, they're like, thank you and then the window closes, and that's it.

There's no streamers or balloons. No-one knocks on your door and congratulates you.

They don't. So I might buy some streamers!

Please film that and send it to us! What do you think your best money habit is?

My best money habit is that I can get a bargain anywhere and I make money work for me in every way I can. I'm not a stinge, but I always look for the best deal.

And what's your worst money habit?

Giving gifts is my love language. And although I budget for it, I don't think I budget enough. Because I don't live very close to my family and friends, I can't just do free things for them, so I'm often sending them gifts or flowers or buying them experiences. And that's obviously not cheap.

That's really sweet, though. That's not the worst habit.

But I do need to be more realistic. Instead of sending flowers, maybe let's switch that out to just a nice note or something.

Obviously you've come a long way and have been through a huge amount. What would you say now to baby you, at age 15?

I was terrified at the time, especially because I was really close with my dad. I felt like I was losing my best friend. My 15-year-old self probably wouldn't have wanted to hear this as everything was so horrible at the time, but in hindsight, it was probably the best thing that's ever happened to me. It forced me to learn how to be independent – to not rely on anyone, but learn how to do everything on my own and pay my own way. I think it taught me that I'm capable of overcoming anything. My older siblings had been spoon fed to the point that when they moved out of home, their rent was paid. They found it really hard to come out of that mindset. I'm almost glad it happened to me when I was younger, because it forced me to just go out and do it all myself. I know I'll always earn my own money and I don't want anyone to ever have that over me.

I don't mean to generalise, but you're a beautiful woman who's just had her dream wedding. If people see this on Instagram or on Facebook they might think it's all been handed to you on a silver platter. Obviously they don't know your family's story because it's none of their damn business, but the reality is that you did this all yourself. Yet, do you find that people still see you as entitled?

Yeah, people look at me and my husband and think we've just got lucky, that we must earn lots of money. It's the same with fitness. People see someone with a strong, muscular body and think it must be really easy. Well, no, actually it's really hard work. They don't know my past, because I don't tell anyone about it. I don't want their judgement and I don't want them to think of me in a different way. But the reality is, you just never know what's happened in people's lives to get them to where they are.

Yes, I am privileged, because I have a loving family who always sticks by each other. But we did have everything taken away from us, and we did have to try and save the day, which hasn't been great. It's taken a while, but I've slowly come to the point where I feel like I'm in control of my finances and I'm on top of it and it's all on me.

The buck stops with you.

Exactly. The more successful you are, the more you work towards things – the wedding, the house, organising all of this stuff – the more people just automatically assume that you must be privileged. But it's all about putting your head down and getting the work done.

So now you're a business development manager and you make six figures and you're killing it. Your super's looking really sexy. You have an online side hustle. You just paid off your wedding in cash. You have $55,000 in super. And you're only $1500 away from being debt free. Do you really think you're only a B plus?

Yeah, I'm still a B plus. I could be doing more. I want to invest more in shares and I want to be investing consistently.

Raised Rich, Now $17K in Debt!

This money diarist puts paid to the belief that money necessarily equals contentment. Coming from a wealthy family for whom money was never an issue, her childhood was a life of privilege. But after leaving home and school early to start working in fashion, she got herself into significant debt. Now married, at age 24, she's learning how to navigate life on her own terms, manage her finances *and* have healthier relationships.

What grade would you give your money habits?

Probably a B minus.

Tell us about your money story.

Okay, well, I was adopted by a really well-off family when I was about 18 months old. Growing up, everything was pretty excessive. I never really went without and I would have had more than the average person, which was great, I guess. I went to a private school and did all the extracurricular activities. But when I turned 18 and was allowed some more freedom, I got my own credit card and quickly got myself into about $17,000 worth of debt. I wasn't working a hugely well-paying job at the time, only about $50,000, so compared to my salary, the minimum repayments were huge.

How did you rack up $17,000 in debt?

I'd been so used to having everything and had this mentality of, if I want it, I can have it and there are no ramifications. Even to the point where I didn't realise you had to pay debt off! My dad was so generous when we were kids – everything we'd put in our bank account each year, he'd double. I look back now and I'm just annoyed at myself. I mainly spent money on silly things, like clothes and handbags and expensive holidays. I was lucky I got to study in France for a year, so that's where a lot of my debt came from. I also love art and my house is adorned with art that I really couldn't afford to buy at the time.

But things changed? How?

I started a relationship with my now husband and, eventually, I told him. He comes from a completely different financial background, had grown up with the bare minimum, so he taught me how to use my money better and to be a bit more mindful.

One day, when we were with my family on holiday in New Zealand, my husband said, I don't want to see you struggle anymore. I'll help you clear your debt and we can start fresh together.

I'd already paid down a big portion of the debt and he wanted to help me clear the slate. He wrote out a little contract that said,

This is a gift. If ever you feel like you want to pay it back and you can, that's up to you. But I'm not expecting it.

Oh, what a dream guy!

It was incredible, but at the time it was hard to accept, because I was locked in this pride bubble. I was in such a weird position. I'd been given everything, but had thrown a large portion of it away, and then found myself being helped by someone who'd grown up with less than me. I just felt so uncomfortable.

But he was so kind, so we just started from ground zero. We put together a plan; what we wanted for the future. I should also say at this point that I have a trust fund, so part of the debt will eventually be paid out of that, but I can't access it just yet.

Tell us a bit more about your adoption.

I was actually born in Fiji and adopted when I was 18 months old. My parents were there on business and I guess they decided to bring back a souvenir!

They weren't planning on adopting. My mum was pregnant at the time, but she had a miscarriage. They were in Fiji for two years and then the coup happened. My dad had to come back to Australia, but my mum stayed on for a bit. She was helping out at a charity one day when my biological mum came along with her friend and little-baby me. My mum was totally entranced. She says that within two days of seeing me she just knew she was meant to be my mum.

And your biological mum agreed with that? Do you have any relationship with her now?

My biological mum needed the money and it took a financial burden off her shoulders. I have other biological siblings in Fiji, but I don't have anything to do with them or my birth mother. I am a lot younger them and my birth wasn't planned.

When I was brought back to Australia, most of my new family accepted me. But a few wondered about the money, since my family's very wealthy, and whether I should be included in the wills and that sort of thing. My great-grandmother was really wealthy and she left a lot of money to her sons. My grandmother decided that each grandchild would have a trust fund and she's been investing on our behalf for years.

Oh gosh, that sounds messy. Did that make it hard when you were growing up, to ask your parents for things because you were adopted?

No, no. They never made me feel different. I'm one of three kids and it's always been an equal playing field. If anything, they gave me more. They were probably overcompensating. I've had a credit card forever and it was always just a normal part of life. I didn't really understand how they worked.

My grandmother is a baller and that's why it makes me feel so ashamed to have gotten myself into all that debt. The way the trust is set up is probably a good thing. I can't access the trust fund until my nan dies. And then I have to put a proposal forward to my parents. My dad is the executor, so he's the one who'll release the funds, but only for investments. Five years ago it was about $800,000, so it's probably sitting at just over $1 million now.

So it sounds like things changed once you met you partner. What happened between your partner helping with your debt and getting married?

Just a lot of education, really! We worked really hard and we managed to buy two properties in the same year as getting married. And we got married overseas, which was amazing.

Most of our friends were really happy for us. But it's hard sometimes because you have to watch what you say. It's not relatable right now saying how much you spend, because a lot of people are really struggling. You can't just blurt shit out.

So has it negatively impacted your friendships?

As my parents have gotten wealthier, it's become more and more obvious with cars and boats and that sort of thing, and it's become difficult to maintain some friendships because some people can't help comparing – they want you to sit just above or below them. So I find that really awkward.

Even when it comes to a job, I have actively decided *not* to work for my parents' company. But the moment you tell people where you live or what you do on the weekend, they can't quite believe it. You feel like an imposter, weirdly. So I usually tone it down.

It totally makes sense. But it sucks that you have to tone yourself down to make other people comfortable.

Yeah, there's a bit of that. And I'm only 24, so some people get really irked.

You said you didn't want to work for your parents' company, so what do you do and how much money do you earn?

I do fashion design and I earn about $95,000 plus super. I left school in year 10. I was lucky – you know how they do work experience? I was offered a job with a fashion house, so I did that and they paid for my training, so fashion's all I know, really.

That makes a lot more sense about your debt being a lot of designer fashion – it's quite common in your industry. I feel there's a theme here.

Oh yeah, there's a big one. You should see my handbag collection!

Alright, tell us about some of your big money goals.

We want to buy our big family home. We're currently in a three-bedroom house in Sydney, but we want to buy a five- to six-bedroom home on or near the water. We're currently looking at something around $3 million, but it's a five-to-six year goal.

How are you going to finance that? How much does your partner earn?

He earns $200,000.

Okay, that's great. And will you need family support as well?

With the equity in our homes, we should be able to use that for the deposit, but we'll also probably look at applying for a portion of my trust to be released.

What about other goals? Holidays? Babies?

I want both! I've also done some modelling. I took a break from that during COVID, but I'd like to get back into it next year.

How exciting. Tell us about your investments.

My husband and I have two properties. I count the property we live in as an investment, although I know it's not technically one, but we bought it purely for investment reasons. The original goal was to stay in it for five years, then buy our big home. But at the same time, we wondered, with all the government grants, what else can we do? My husband's in engineering, so he's very good with numbers. He thought we'd be better off if we had two properties instead of just one big one right now. So we've got where we live now – the loan's about $600,000 on that place, but it's worth about $950,000. And our investment property – the loan is at $580,000 and that's worth just under $900,000. And we also have about $25,000 in shares.

What process did you follow to pick your shares?

It just started as a hobby. It seemed everyone was doing it, so I signed up to an online platform that my friends recommended – their market round-ups make it really easy. I'm mostly invested in ETFs. Once they've grown to a certain target, after taking into account any capital gains tax, I sell up and transfer the proceeds into my bigger portfolio.

And what about debts, other than the mortgages?

Instead of paying stamp duty on our investment property in NSW, we opted to pay land tax, so we hold a debt to cover that – around $47,000. I also use Afterpay, but only for gifts and clothing. I've got about $500 sitting in that.

What do you think your best money habit is?

Probably, that I'm organised. When I need to buy something – birthday presents and that sort of thing – I'll make sure I get it at a really good price.

And your worst money habit?

I think it's linked to being raised in excess in a wealthy household – basically spending too much, although that's mostly in the past. My parents used to pay for everything; bills, my car, my phone. But once I started working, they told me I had to start buying my own clothes because they're expensive. And same with artworks. So I was spending like I used to, but only earning $50,000 and that's where the debt started.

Then, there's this understanding in my family that once you're married, it's all on you. So now that I'm married, I have to be more responsible. But it's hard, because my parents are still spending like they've always done. We're going overseas with them next year to Japan and they offered to pay for everything except for the accommodation. Which sounds great, but if I pay for accommodation where they're staying, it'll be like $8500 for four nights!

So how do you have these conversations with them?

It can be icky. There are times where I just can't be bothered to even discuss it because I just feel uncomfortable and I know they're going to want to pay for it if I say something. And yeah, that is privilege and I'm incredibly lucky to have parents in that position, but sometimes you just feel embarrassed. I don't want to have to explain it to them like I'm a five year old.

So they're paying for everyone to fly business class when we go to Japan, but because I'm now married, they said I can either share my ticket fare with my husband and we both fly economy or stump up the extra to go business class. Which feels weird, because it's not like one extra business class ticket would impact them. I mean, they pay on points, they don't ever pay for flights. So it's confusing. My brother literally didn't work for five years and only just started working and he's only ever flown business class.

It sounds super uncomfortable around your parents because of these little things. Maybe they're trying to teach you some financial independence but in a really weird way?

I don't know. I brought it up with my therapist and she thought it was bizarre.

Is this something you knew would happen if you got married?

I did know. I just didn't know how terrible it would feel. And my mum doesn't really get it. For example, I've been going to the same skin therapist as my mum forever. But then I was like, I actually can't afford that, it's $250 an hour. So I cancelled my appointment, but later, Mum asks how my facial was. So I tell her, well no, I didn't go to her, I can't afford it. And she says, oh, you're so cheap! And I want to be like, I don't have your income! But it's too hard.

If my sister's in the room, we'll both give each other a look and I'll just roll my eyes. Sometimes it's just not worth the argument. I know it's such a small insignificant thing, but it adds up, you know? It's not just a one-time thing where your mum calls you cheap because you changed your facialist, it's like, your entire lifestyle has changed. So the hurt and discomfort kind of compounds. It just goes on and on and on.

She's *on the* Money

Conversations around money can be difficult, no matter which side of the fence you're coming from, especially among family or old friends that carry certain expectations around past you.

When you're trying to change your money story but meeting a lot of resistance, it can be worthwhile to work with a counsellor or psychologist to help you gain perspective and maintain your conviction.

If your mental health is suffering, try speaking with your GP as they may be able to arrange a bulk-billed mental health care plan to cover the cost of your appointments.

So how are you managing now? Are you learning to live within your means?

I find holiday seasons awful. I always overspend, there's just an expectation that you will in our family. But I just need to budget more or put more money towards that and be more mindful. But in regards to the other things, I'm learning to find cheaper alternatives that I enjoy.

Do you still think you're a B minus? If so, why, and how would you change to get to an A?

Yeah, I still think I'm a B minus. I need to change my relationship with money – and my relationship with people with money – so I can feel more confident in my decisions and feel at peace with them. I know that I overspend because sometimes I feel like I have to please people. I want to eventually get to a point where I don't have to feel that way. That's when I'll be like, okay, yeah, you're moving up, girl!

Scammed by Her Own Fam

This money diarist is a 33-year-old married doctor who got scammed $271,000 by her own cousin! Nice one, cuz. Thankfully, she's managed to pull herself out of the financial hellhole thanks to a lot of hard graft, but friends, let her story be a warning . . . it can happen to anyone.

I want to know so much about this, but before we get into it, how would you grade your money habits?

Probably a B plus.

Okay. Now, tell us a bit about your money story.

Growing up, I didn't have much financial literacy. Money wasn't talked about in our family; it was all adult affairs, hush hush. I learnt to not ask my parents about their jobs or how much they earnt. I was also made to feel like it was a bad thing to accept gifts or money on birthdays or special events because you weren't meant to be taking money from others, you were meant to be saving your own money.

I didn't start working until I was 19, so I had no concept of superannuation or tax until then. And even then, working while at uni, I didn't understand the importance of all those things. I blindly fumbled my way through working a few part-time jobs while I was studying. Even when I started working as a doctor, I just earnt, spent and saved, but I didn't know what I was saving for and I didn't really know how to save, so it was just like, whatever I didn't spend ended up as savings, and I was going through that endless cycle. Until I got scammed, that is. That changed my perspective on things.

How did this happen? You seem like a smart, successful person – how does one get scammed out of $271,000?

It didn't happen in one big lump sum, but over a period of about a year and a half. I have family overseas and my cousin's overseas, but I grew up with her, so we had a pretty close relationship when we were kids. It started off when she told me that her boyfriend was in trouble and she needed to help him out. She said it was a one-off thing. So I transferred her some money and that was the start of an ongoing cycle of lies. She told me she couldn't go to anyone else and that I was the only one she could trust.

When the story about her boyfriend had reached its limit, she came up with another story about someone we both knew – a mutual friend – how he was in financial strife and being hounded by loan sharks. I knew the person she was referring to really was in financial strife, so I believed my cousin and didn't question her version of events, even though the stories got more and more weird. For example, she told me she needed me to pay for his medical expenses because he was unwell. Then she told me his mother had died, so she needed more money. In the back of my mind, I did wonder what I was doing and why this was happening, but I never actually spoke to the person she was referring to. It was always through my cousin. I blindly trusted her.

Because she was a close family member.

Exactly. So it just kept going until it reached this point where it was becoming ridiculous. I was getting random messages from random phone numbers I didn't recognise, harassing me for money. And when I questioned her about it, there were more lies. So I stopped giving her money. I'd picked up a few clues along the way that led me to believe it might be a scam. When I stopped giving her money, she changed her story again, and I then realised it really was all a scam and that I needed to bail. By then, I'd already given her over $270,000.

Oh my gosh, that's awful. I'm so sorry you went through that.

It really wasn't a pleasant time! I took out four credit cards and a personal loan and was working day and night to cover it. The funny thing was, in the beginning, it wasn't even about the money – I was just earning it, then funnelling it to her. But it just escalated. Once I realised what was happening and started getting help, I finally reached my point of no return. I knew I was never going to go back to that cycle.

How did you broach it with your family?

It's really awkward, still. I reached out to her parents and asked them whether all of this was true. I don't know if that was a mistake or not, because they ended up taking her side and said that I was lying. Thankfully, I had help from other relatives where she lives who did a bit of background snooping, which gave me the evidence I needed. In terms of the money, eventually I received a lot of help from my parents and my friends to get me out of it, but it took me a long time to confess to them. I was just so ashamed of what I'd done and felt like I was the one who'd caused it all. It was really difficult to tell them, but once I did, it was fine.

You obviously don't have a relationship with your cousin anymore, but what are things like in the broader family?

I haven't seen my cousin or heard from her since I confronted her and told her I knew she was lying. She's basically blocked me and her parents have blocked me and they've cut off all contact from the rest of the family as well. No-one really knows what's happened to them and where she is or what she's doing.

I sought legal options to try and get the money back, but it felt like I'd just be throwing good money after bad. So, in the end, I thought it wasn't worth it. I've now paid off all the debts I accumulated in that period, so that's good. It took me about three years to get completely debt-free after the whole saga, so a slow process, but finally the slate has been wiped cleaned.

I'm so glad you're not still stuck in that mess. You said you and your cousin were close. Were there any red flags growing up that maybe she wasn't the most honest person, or did this just come out of the blue?

On reflection, there were some indicators. She's a bit older than me and I used to see her lie sometimes. Sometimes she ensured I got the blame for something I never did, but I just put that down to childhood immaturity. I never took it seriously. Looking back, there were some things that hinted, I guess, at her unbecoming character. As an adult, as things started to become complex and the lies increased, I worked out that what she was saying didn't stack up.

She's *on the* Money

Everybody assumes that to be scammed you have to be silly, or unintelligent, or unable to see things. But scammers are experts at what they do and have all sorts of technology at their fingertips. They use both emotional and intelligence systems to manipulate you. If they know you, they have access to even more insights and knowledge to undermine you. They rely on your trust in the relationship that they've created with you. Normal people aren't trained to think and behave like that, let alone detect it.

There is often a lot of stigma attached to being duped and victims often feel shame that somehow they 'allowed' it to happen. But if you don't have full access to the facts, you can't make sensible decisions. Instead, you rely on what you've been told or think you know. Here, our diarist acted because she cared and is a kind human being who wanted her cousin and this other person to be okay. There is no shame in kindness. And feeling shame for being manipulated? Well, it's clear that the person doing the manipulating is in the wrong here. Taking advantage of someone's heart, that's the lowest.

To help protect yourself from these situations, double-check the facts and verify them independently. If someone's telling you a story, confirm it directly with the source, if they're 'sick' speak to their doctor, if it's an 'insurance company' check their licence and details. Search the internet for the kinds of phrases they're using or promises they're making. Online chat boards are filled with stories from people sharing similar stories.

How did you reach out for help?

I reached out to a different cousin. I kept calling the number of the mutual friend who was in trouble but he never answered the phone, which is obviously a massive red flag. So I called a different cousin who then managed to get the guy's real number and I managed to get through to him. He had no idea that his name was being used in this way. He might have been lying as well, but I don't think he was. I think he was just the scapegoat.

That was after about a year or so of being manipulated. It took me another six months to tell my mum. It was one of those things that was so complex and unbelievable that I couldn't verbalise it, so I wrote her a long letter so she could get the facts before losing her mind!

What did your parents say when they found out? Obviously this was their niece, so how did they feel about it?

They were really surprised and shocked. At first, my mum was angry at me for being deceived and being so gullible. She was also angry at my cousin, but when she confronted her, my cousin just lied again. That was when my mum realised the extent of what had happened to me and how much I'd been manipulated. Although she wasn't happy that it had occurred, she helped me get rid of some of my debt.

I'm so glad you had your parents. And also, let's realise that this is just something that happened to you along your financial journey and not the defining factor! Tell us more about you. What do you do for work? How much money do you earn?

I'm a doctor. I work in a hospital and do private work as well, so I have about four streams of income. My total income varies because of the private work, but last financial year I earnt just under $25,000 a month pre-tax which works out to around $13,000 a month after tax. I divide that into savings, splurge and expenses that I share with my husband.

Very impressive. What is your big money goal? What are we working towards?

I recently hit my previous money goal, which was to buy a house. So that's done! My next money goal is saving for when I'm not able to work, like for maternity leave, and also saving for investments to grow our wealth.

You've been through the wars, but it sounds like you're coming out the other side. You're back on track, out of debt and have purchased your first home, which is so exciting. Working towards your next big money goals, what are your investment plans for the future?

I've already got an investment property and some shares, but the longer term plan is to invest for our future children's education and also to grow our wealth generally, to the point of generating a passive income, so I don't have to work as much. Every month we're putting aside a certain amount of money to invest in shares. The idea is to invest over the next 15 years or so and hopefully build a portfolio.

My husband is obsessed with our future kids going to private schools and that's going to be a significant cost. I don't share the same beliefs about a private school education, though. I went to a private school and my school was fantastic, but I don't have anything to compare it to, so I think that public school in Australia could potentially be just as good.

We're pretty open about discussing everything. We do the whole date night thing where we talk about money-related stuff, review our goals and our savings and budget.

Great, the most important things is to keep talking so you can be on the same page. Now, what debts do you have?

I have zero personal debt, credit card debt or HECS debt. In terms of the investment property, I have a $430,000 mortgage. On the place where we live, my husband and I share a $1.33 million mortgage.

At 33, you're quite young and killing it! When did you get your investment property and what led you down the path of making the decision to purchase that?

My investment property was my principal place of residence at the time I bought it off the plan back in 2018. The funny thing is that while I was getting scammed, I still knew that I had to pay my mortgage repayments above anything else. So I never defaulted on that, but I just didn't have money for anything else, basically! I was living there and then, when my husband and I decided to move in together, he had the funds for a deposit already saved and I had the borrowing capacity. So we managed to get a property together in both our names and that's when my other place turned into an investment property.

Your $1.33 million mortgage leaves a bit of a lump in my throat. How did you feel taking out a mortgage that big?

We saw a lot of properties in the area so we'd done a lot of research beforehand. We had a good mortgage broker and bought below our pre-approval max, so when we did buy, we were comfortable that we could make the repayments. But we bought just before the first lot of interest rates went up. Since then, every time we think we know what our monthly repayment amount will be, it just goes up again. Thankfully, we didn't stretch our borrowing capacity – we borrowed just under.

What do you think is your best money habit?

Probably setting up direct debits for bills so I don't have to think about it and it's all automated. Also, setting up my savings buckets in the first place because, before, there was no structure to anything, so I didn't know what I was doing. Now I feel more in control and can see when savings get built up over time which is really satisfying.

What do you think is your worst money habit?

I'm a bit stingy with allocating money for myself for splurge and discretionary expenses. I end up digging into other funds to make something happen and then have to keep transferring money back and forth to even it out afterwards.

It sounds like you've gone through a lot. Obviously being scammed by your cousin is unthinkable. But you've come out the other side, met your husband, moved in together, have a family home together, you have your own investment property, you're investing, you're saving, you have a bang-on cashflow system. Do you really think that you're only a B plus?

Yes. Because I still have more learning to do in terms of things like insurance, asset protection and wealth creation. There's a whole lot of terminology that I still don't understand and I would like to learn more about. I was probably an F a few years ago, so I think I've come a long way!

She's *on the* Money

Cashflow is one of my favourite things ever. It's actually so fun when things start to work, watching where things are going and which bucket they're going to fall into and being able to project forward, to see that your goals are going to be achieved. There's just such a sense of accomplishment in that.

I have a fully laid out cashflow system in my first book, *She's on the Money*, but essentially, it's setting up a series of accounts to help manage and keep track of different parts of your finance: from income, to saving, to spending, and always, an emergency fund.

When people tell me their best habit is cashflow, I'm like, yeah! Go get it! A good cashflow system will set you up for life. It's the best thing you can do for yourself, regardless of what you earn.

DEBT JOURNALLING PROMPTS

Write out a list of all the debts you owe, from personal loans to credit cards to pay later schemes, as well as any mortgages or investment loans.

Have you got a plan for repaying these? If not, the free Basic Budget Template on our website is a good place to start. Download this resource then write out some target dates for getting your budgeting and cashflow in order.

List out all the 'extra' things you should be budgeting for, like friends' birthdays, health check-ups and insurances.

Write out your plan for celebrating the day you become debt free!

Debt Money Wins

REBECCA was considering what to do with some extra money she had saved and, after crunching some numbers, opted to pay off her car loan. She calculated that by paying it off early she would save over $3500 in interest and account fees.

JULIE took a leap and pooled all of her excess funds together to pay off her credit card debt. She used a small amount from her emergency fund but made sure to leave a greater amount than her credit limit in there as back-up. Her aim is to boost her emergency fund further and cancel the credit card.

After lots of financial re-evaluating, **MIRANDA** paid off, cancelled and cut up her credit card. She'd found it too easy to overspend, so getting rid of it helped her feel liberated.

JULIA turned to Facebook Marketplace to earn some extra cash to help pay off her buy now, pay later balance. Once maxed out, her balance is now halved. She also started adding $5 to each of her bank accounts every pay day for some extra savings wins.

EMILY did some detective work on her own spending habits and calculated that over the past two and half years she had spent $9,100 on Afterpay purchases. It shocked her to realise that a lot of her purchases were non-essential and that she could have paid off her debt with that amount – and then some. Rather than getting upset about it, she took it as an opportunity to reflect and chose not to feel embarrassed by her choices. Now she's ready to take even more control over her money!

TEGAN accumulated a *lot* of debt in her early twenties – we're talking $50,000 worth. Now, she has paid off her last $1000 of debt. She also had buy now, pay later accounts which she closed down two years ago. In her own words, she worked her butt off to pay back every single cent of her consumer debt – and she did it! And now Tegan can finally work towards her goal of purchasing a dream home.

Announcement! **RACHELLE** is now a debt-free woman! She has had a complicated relationship with money and grew up in a household with lots of money troubles. In adulthood she found herself in a long-term relationship with a partner who also had less than ideal money habits, and soon got herself into a significant amount of personal debt. But she felt empowered to start paying it off after her bestie recommended the SOTM podcast. Over the past year, she has worked hard to pay off $13,000 in debt – and she's left the relationship. Her first step? Paying off her credit card debt with a small amount of savings. Onwards and upwards!

KATIE'S big money win is that she is officially car-debt free. The minimum repayment was $250 per fortnight, and while she didn't have a ridiculously high income she still committed to paying as much as she could afford. She redirected her emergency fund allocation towards paying it off. Now that her debt's cleared, she's doubling down on rebuilding her emergency fund.

NICOLE saved *super hard* for the past six months and managed to pay off her HECS debt before the latest indexation! She was so proud of herself, she cried!

AMBER was eager to get her debt cleared quicker, so she got a second job. Now she's earning an extra $800 to $1000 per week, which is going to massively help her power through.

Property

As a nation, Australians have typically been passionate about creating wealth through property. And though I actively encourage our community to pursue financial growth across all avenues, from career to investments, there's no doubt that property fulfils both financial and emotional wellbeing goals. While many feel that a property dream is far out of reach, our community is filled with stories from millennials who've started from nothing and are now smashing their property goals.

While my third book, *Property with She's on the Money*, is chock-full of detailed information on how to go about chasing your property dream, these diarists share some fresh inspo and inside intel on how they've managed to crack this golden egg. So strap in and get comfy as dreams really do come true!

Growing Up With Nothing to Owning Her Own Home

This money diarist came from a low-income, single-parent household and suffered emotional and physical abuse. But she worked her way through TAFE, earning three certificates and two diplomas, and then went to uni. After a shock split with her partner, she lost the land they'd bought together, as well as a contract they had to build a house, but she regrouped and, shortly after, bought a unit on her own. At 25 years old, she's definitely on her way back and then some!

First question, what is your attitude towards money?

Growing up, it was just me and my mum. She worked as a teacher's aide in school, which didn't earn very much, but she managed to have a mortgage on her own. She was always saying we didn't have enough money. So I had that 'scarcity mindset' really early on.

When I moved out of home, I realised I didn't want to struggle like that and I didn't want to stress about money all the time. It really affected my mum's mental health. As a kid I was quite embarrassed at the supermarket because we had to use food stamps, though at the time I didn't fully realise the extent of her struggles and the pressure she was under.

Do you know anything about her money story?

Yes, I do and it's really interesting because I think it's a generational thing. My grandma came from Hungary and worked five jobs to support her three kids. They were all under five when they came to Australia and they had to get jobs when they were just 10 years old to help support the family. My mum bought a house really young, with my dad, but then she got breast cancer just before I was born, and it all went downhill from there. She went from doing well financially and setting herself up, to struggling mentally with the cancer diagnosis, so I think she started buying things to kind of fill the void. When I was growing up, even though she was on a pretty low income and trying to pay the mortgage and all the other bills, she'd go and buy lots of material things. From a young age, I wondered why she was doing that. I couldn't understand why someone would be buying all these items they never even touched, when instead they could be paying off a mortgage and not be worried.

She's *on the* Money

This is a great example of why I talk so much about money stories. Often money stories are inherited and come in generational cycles, so it can take a lot of awareness and conscious decision-making to change your money story.

The first step is acknowledging where your money thoughts and behaviours might have come from, asking yourself, why do I feel like that about money? Why does it really frustrate me or why does it make me feel sick?

If it's because that's how you grew up, then that makes a lot of sense. There's no shame in money stories because they're not our fault. No-one chooses their initial money story, but the cool thing about them is that, as an adult, once you become aware, you can choose what to do with them. Once you know your money story you can choose to change it.

What do you do for work and how much money do you earn?

I was a disability support worker for five years but I injured my back when I was 21. Since that work kept aggravating the injury, I knew I had to get out, although it took me four years to do so! At the moment, I'm working from home with an NDIS provider and I'm really enjoying it. In my old job, last year I earnt about $74,000, but I was doing a lot of weekends, a lot of sleepovers, a lot of public holidays. It was too much. I'm now 25 and have wised up. For my current role, I took a pay cut and I'm now on about $52,000.

As carers, we often put ourselves last. I'm glad to hear you've prioritised your own mental and physical health now – that's even more important than money. And now that you're looking after yourself, what is your big money goal?

I've got more than one! I place a lot of emphasis on goals and I guess that's how I've got to this point. But at the moment, it's mainly just paying extra off the mortgage and building up my investment portfolio. I want financial freedom and I want the option to retire early. So, that's my big goal.

Can you tell us what that means exactly?

For me, it's not necessarily about retiring at a specific age, but more about having the option to do so, or even just to go part-time and do more travel or volunteering.

So it's about having the financial freedom to make those decisions?

Yeah, absolutely.

Do you currently have any investments?

I have super which is about $43,000 at the moment. I haven't started contributing extra yet – I was saving for my house, so I kind of put super on the back burner.

That's a good amount in super for your age. How old were you when you got your first job?

I was 14 and nine months when I got my first job, at KFC.

Okay, that makes sense. When you start working really early, you also start contributing to super so that can build up really nicely. What other investments do you have?

I've got some shares – ETFs in listed investment companies (LICs) – so there's about $14,000 in my accounts there at the moment too. One of my goals is to build that up.

Do you currently have any debts?

As part of my upbringing and having that scarcity mindset, I paid all my uni fees up front. My values are aligned to just not having any debt at all. So it's pretty much just the mortgage on my unit.

And how much is your mortgage?

It's currently about $370,000.

What does that mean for your cashflow? How much are you paying each month?

My minimum payments are pretty much what I was paying in rent, so that's really cool. It just made it work it for me in the current market. I know it's a big risk to buy property at such high prices, but I weighed up all the extra fees and crunched the numbers. At the moment I'm putting in about $400 a fortnight extra.

Oh, epic. Congratulations. Can you tell us how much your unit cost and how much of a deposit you were able to save?

I had a $50,000 deposit and the unit was $429,000, so my mortgage came in at about $382,000 when it all settled. Previously, I had put a lot of money into some land I bought with my ex-partner. Over a year and a half we paid down about $80,000, so we only had about $50,000 left on the loan. When we sold the land we got really lucky, because land values don't always go up that much and it was regional as well, but the market was good and we were lucky to sell well, so I got back what I put in. That's where my deposit came from.

What do you think is your best money habit?

I think my best money habit is setting achievable goals and following through on them. I'm a real stickler for goals, but also making sure that they're actually attainable. Obviously, if you set yourself something that you just can't follow through on, you're going to feel pretty crappy and you're not going to feel accomplished. I also think my mindset has helped me avoid getting into substantial debt. It's really important to have those little goals but also make them achievable.

I couldn't agree more. How do you set attainable goals?

Well, when I needed to do some work on my unit, I basically just broke the costs down and worked out what could I afford each week and how long it was going to take me to pay it back. If I hadn't had enough money, I would have deferred the work until I did.

Great. And what's your worst money habit?

I am very harsh on myself if things have to change and I'm not very lenient with myself when it comes to my goals. In the past, if life circumstances changed, for example, if my income shrank (as it did recently), I'd get really stressed and rigidly stick to my goals instead of responding flexibly to the reality of what was happening. I'm trying to work on that inner stuff and being okay with where I'm at and not being so harsh and critical of where I want to go.

If we forced you to give your money habits a grade, what would you grade them?

I would probably say an A minus – mainly thanks to too many takeaway meals! My takeaway food habit just went off the rails during the COVID lockdowns and I really don't love cooking either.

I want to know more about your background and your money story and how that's impacted you as an adult. You've radically changed your personal situation. You've gone from growing up in a world where money was really tight, living paycheque to paycheque and using food stamps, to now, owning your own home. Does your upbringing still impact you day to day?

It was a big factor in why I wanted to buy a house. It's one of the biggest needs for a human, really – having a roof over your head. So I've carried that mindset through, but I feel like it's been positive as well. I have my mum to thank for that in the sense that it's driven me and helped me create my goals and work towards those things. My childhood made me realise I don't want to have those sorts of struggles and I don't want others to have them either.

How's your mum doing now?

She's good, even though she's still a massive hoarder! But she's a legend and she has a really high income at the moment, so she's paying down her mortgage. I'm trying to convince her to pay it off before retirement because she's getting to that age and she hasn't thought about it.

Being a hoarder is quite common when you've grown up in poverty. Once you do have a higher income and financial security you want to hold onto things and not let them go. Do you think that creeps into your money story?

No, I'm actually the opposite. I don't like clutter. I don't like having things in the house unless they're sentimental to me. It stresses me out having too much stuff. I guess that helps in terms of financial goals, because I'm not buying materialistic things all the time. I bought a phone three years ago for about $200 and I dropped it – so it's got a cracked screen – but it still works. My friends keep telling me to buy a new one, but I don't think I need to. They don't get it!

I'm actually trying to work through that a bit more. The more comfortable I get financially, the more I'm learning to relax and buy things that I want and not worry as much.

You mentioned before that you sold some land that you and your ex-partner had bought together. How did that happen and how did you protect yourself?

I was with my ex for nearly five years and we'd been together for four years when we bought the land. At the time, we obviously thought it was going to be a long-term term thing, as everyone does. I didn't get any sort of legal protection because we went into the contract 50/50. I invested more money than him at the start, but he ended up paying more of the mortgage over the year and a half. So we ended up about equal. I wouldn't recommend our setup though, because it's a risk. If the contract says 50/50 and you've put in more upfront and something goes wrong, you might not get all of your money back. But that's what I did and luckily it worked out for me. It wasn't a huge sum of money either, so I guess I kind of weighed up the risk in that sense.

After we bought the land, we signed contracts to build a house on it. We'd picked out everything, cupboards, it was all done, signed, deposit paid, locked in. About two weeks later he told me he couldn't go through with it. He had this childhood trauma come up and it completely ruined him. It was really extreme and it was horrible. He just wanted to be back with his family. They were interstate and with all the lockdowns and everything, he hadn't seen them in so long, and his mum got really sick. Suddenly, he couldn't cope and was just like, I can't do this, we have to get out of it!

I couldn't see that we had any choice, but I wondered how we'd get our money back from the builders. We'd paid the deposit. It was locked in. But luckily it was the right time to sell land. We broke even with all the costs that we put into it and split it amicably. I was lucky that he was really relaxed about it. Looking back, I wish I'd have engaged my broker. I didn't think I'd have the borrowing power to buy him out, so I didn't even look into it. At the time, it was all just so stressful and I just wanted it sorted. But I should have checked.

Do you think that you would have been able to buy him out if you'd had that conversation?

Yes. With all the regional and first home owner loan grants, I would've come out very nicely with a brand-new house on a big property. But that's the joy of hindsight, isn't it? I didn't get any grants with the unit that I bought. Next time, no matter what, I will definitely engage the banks or the broker just to see where I'm at. It's really important.

I'm a genuine believer that everything works out for the best and everything works out for a reason. And it was a pretty shitty situation.

He'd been struggling with his mental health pretty much the whole time I was with him. So I guess in that sense it wasn't a huge shock that he wanted to get out of the relationship.

She's *on the* Money

That's one of the reasons why, when going into a big purchase with somebody else, you must set really clear exit guidelines. I'm not saying this because I'm negative about relationships, but let me ask you: What happens if it doesn't work out and you've sunk a lot into it?

You both need to ask yourselves the tough questions before the bad thing happens. If we break up (or worse), are we going to keep the house or the land? Are we going to own it together or are we going to sell it? Are we going to wait until the market recovers? What if the market isn't doing well? How would one of us cover the mortgage if the other was no longer contributing to it?

If you haven't thought these things through, and the worst comes to pass, you may lose a significant amount of money. It's so important, if you're in a relationship, to have these conversations before it happens.

How are you going to protect yourself in the event that you get into another relationship into the future?

I think it's hard with Australian legislation – with de facto relationships, you're locked in, even if you're not married. I know there's a lot of mixed opinions about binding financial agreements, prenups, that sort of thing, but I'd still rather put the money in to get one drawn up, even if it didn't hold up later on. At least it's proof of your intention. I'm definitely going to be aware that if I do meet someone, if they're staying over, or if they're paying for things around the house, that could all be counted as contributions, which means they could end up having a stake in my property. It's important to have those tough conversations up front.

Ex-defence and on the Property Ladder

Our money diarist is 35 years old, ex-defence and has been on the Queensland property rollercoaster for just over 10 years – riding the highs and lows of the market and dealing with the inevitable issues that arise. But she's worked very hard and is well on the way to becoming fiscally fabulous – even down to tracking her net worth every month!

Tell us a bit about your money story, in particular, your property journey.

I bought my first property in 2012. It was an apartment and it cost me $325,000. I sold it in 2018 for $510,000. It should have been closer to $550,000, but there was a big strata bill coming for works in the complex so I took that off my selling price.

I then used the profits from that place for the deposit for my current house. I then bought an investment property in 2014 for $340,000, but unfortunately, the city it was in didn't do so great. I sold it in 2018 for $265,000. I was gutted. I even had to pay the bank back a little bit of money. In reviewing my research, I probably shouldn't have bought it.

Why did you decide to sell it when you did?

There were two reasons: I had bad tenants and had to kick them out after they'd done $20,000 worth of damage. After the repairs – which were covered by landlord insurance, thankfully – I just couldn't get anyone in to rent it. So I was covering two mortgages. And then on top of that, I was leaving the military and looking to purchase my current house and I just couldn't afford to carry the debt.

It always comes down to the numbers with me. I looked at what my options were if I held onto the place, what my borrowing capacity would be for my next purchase, and how long I could afford to keep untenanted. I weighed everything up and, ultimately, acknowledged it would be a life lesson and I'd have to take the loss. On the plus-side, I still have that capital loss associated with it to offset any future gains in my investments portfolio.

What happened next?

I bought my current home in 2018 for $773,000. This was my third purchase by the age of 30. It was a big step up, but it was a beautiful house. I had a 20 per cent deposit after I sold the investment property, so I avoided lenders mortgage insurance (LMI). I put about $100,000 into the new place over the first two years doing some upgrades and making it exactly how I wanted it. On the conservative side, the value is around $1.3 million now, but realistically, it's probably more like $1.4 million in the current market. The updates and renovations have helped that, but also, Brisbane's property values have grown like crazy recently.

She's *on the* Money

It's important to keep good records for all your investments, such as shares, property and cryptocurrencies, to help with reporting on investment income, claiming tax deductions and benefitting from capital gains or losses when you sell.

If you sell an investment for more than it cost to buy it, that's a capital gain. Capital gains are taxed at your marginal rate and need to be accounted for in your tax return in the year you sell the investment. If you've held the investment for more than 12 months, you'll qualify for the capital gains tax (CGT) discount, and be taxed on only half of the capital gain.

If you sell an investment for less than it cost to buy it, that's a capital loss. You can use a capital loss to either reduce capital gains made in the year the loss occurs, or carry the loss forward to offset future capital gains, thereby reducing your taxable income in the year they're declared.

So after a small loss on the investment property, you stepped up and bought this really big property. Talk us through your thought process.

You feel completely different when you're looking at somewhere to live versus somewhere to invest, which puts me in a tricky situation with this investment property I'm about to buy. My plan is not to put any cash down and instead borrow completely against the equity in my current property. But in the current market, everybody is trying to buy at that same price point – it's super competitive.

I'm looking at properties around $550,000 and there are a lot of first-home buyers looking as well – which is crazy having to save that much money as a first-home buyer – but they're obviously doing it, and they're passionate about getting their first home.

When I'm looking at an investment, I'm crunching all the numbers as to what I need to outlay, what it's going to cost me, what my rental income might be, and I've obviously got a drop-dead number, because otherwise it doesn't make financial sense. So I'm getting outbid every time, which is a bit frustrating, but really it's fine. Something will come up eventually.

Are you managing this process on your own or do you have a buyer's agent?

I've been looking on my own, though I have considered a buyer's agent, purely to try to find something before it hits the market. I don't have the relationships they have and I feel that's the biggest advantage at the moment, given there are so many passionate first-time buyers out there. But obviously using a buyer's agent is expensive, maybe $10,000, so I'd need to factor that in.

She's *on the* Money

While reasonably new to the Australian property market, buyer's agents are common in the US and becoming increasingly popular here. A buyer's agent is the counterpoint to a property agent. They act on behalf of the buyer, whereas the real estate agent acts on behalf of the seller.

In a hot market, buyer's agents may secure opportunities that are more difficult for an everyday buyer to find. Because they're working full-time in the industry they have established strong relationships with the active agents in the area who'll often give them advance notice of upcoming properties before they come onto the market.

Buyer's agents' clients often get the advantage of seeing a place before it's open to the public, allowing them to make an early offer and giving them more time to get their finances and inspections in order. Plus, the buyer's agent will conduct the negotiations on their client's behalf – and knowing the seller's agent and the area can give them greater leverage.

In a highly competitive market, these advantages could mean the difference between securing a property or not, and in quieter markets, possibly a better price and other beneficial terms.

Do you have any other investments?

I have my military super – I was getting 23 per cent for 10 years. When I left the military five years ago, the balance was about $310,000. I haven't made any additional contributions and it's now around $368,000. When I retire or when I hit retirement age at 57, I'll be entitled to a $17,000 military pension per year until I die. Each military super fund is different, but in my case, they came up with the figure of $17,000 based on the length of my service as well as what my salary was while I was serving.

I also have a second super account with Australian Super because my military super is reserved purely for military pay. That second super account is sitting at $83,000 after five years out in the civilian world. I've been putting in maximum contributions for that as well. So, over $450,000 in super all up.

Nice one. Do you have any other investments?

I'm not sure if you'd classify it as an investment, but sitting on the positive side of my assets, I have around $255,000 in cash. It's currently in the offset account for my house. It's made up of profit from the sale of my last property as well as other savings from my salary, bonuses and tax refunds. I also still do reserve work for the Australian Defence Force. So any money I make from that goes into my little cash pile as well.

My intent is not to touch those savings. I want to fully borrow against the equity in the property as it exists already. My mortgage is currently $495,000, so if the house gets valued at $1.4 million, I'll have just shy of a million dollars in equity.

Talk to us about other investments. Do you invest in shares, for example?

A few years ago I reached out to some financial advisors, but didn't feel like they added much value to what I knew already. I did that again about two months ago and spoke to three different people. The first two didn't feel quite right, but the third was really good. Essentially, he validated a lot of the things I already knew and kept me comfortable with my cash sitting in my offset at 6 per cent.

Looking at investing, when considering market rates and

the tax rate for any profit, personally I'd be wanting to look at a 10 per cent return just to break even on my money, and even with a 10 per cent return, there's still risk. He recommended I start investing small amounts of money in shares to learn and understand the market. He said ETFs were another option, but I wouldn't get the same learning outcomes compared with experimenting on the share market.

I feel like property is what I know at the moment and things have been going up which makes me feel confident, whereas shares or ETFs feel more risky to me and I'm not a super high-risk kind of person.

That is so fine. Do you have any debts?

The short answer is no. I have a credit card, which gets me a lot of Qantas points, but that gets cleared every pay. I've been good with my credit card since learning about the points system. Literally every dollar I spend goes on my credit card: all my bills, all my outgoings. I have a budget, but I probably manage it in a different way to most people. I know what my outgoings are for everything per month, so my mortgage is this, my bills are this, and so on. Whatever's left over, I split into two piles: half for savings, half for fun money. Let's say there's a thousand dollars left at the end of the month, I put $500 into savings and $500 into fun money, so I know that I have that $500 on tap. I don't feel guilty about buying that new dress or going out for drinks or whatever; I've allocated myself that money.

That's very cool. Is that your best money habit, do you think?

Yeah, I think the way I budget and manage my money is pretty good. Splitting it into the savings and fun money and using what's left rather than worrying about particular buckets for holidays or a new car or whatever works really well for me.

The other thing I do, which is pretty nerdy but also pretty exciting, is I track my net worth. My money situation is obviously pretty simple at the moment. I just have my property assets, two super accounts and my cash sitting against my liability – that's my mortgage – and I feed everything into this spreadsheet and it punches out my net worth each month. It helps me keep my eye on what's going on in the world.

This month, my magical net worth is currently $1.512 million.

Oh my gosh, she's a millionaire at 35! What about your worst money habit?

I still need to diversify and be okay with taking some risk. One of my life mottos is 'knowledge is power'. So I just want to continue to learn and understand how things work and how I can make my money work best for me.

Okay, great. And finally, what money grade would you give yourself?

Somewhere around an A. I've still got some things to learn and, don't get me wrong, I still like to treat myself every now and then. So there's always room for improvement. I don't think I'm ever going to know everything, but I definitely want to learn more and share that knowledge and help other people around me as well.

Dairy Farming to Mining and Firefighting

This 28-year-old money diarist grew up on a dairy farm in the NSW Hunter region. After working various hospo jobs, she retrained and moved to the mining sector where she earns very good coin. On the side, she also worked as a casual firefighter, but in a cruel twist of fate, the investment property she'd worked so hard to buy burnt to the ground. She's currently rebuilding, resetting and focusing on the future.

What grade you would give your money habits?

Either an A or a B plus.

Can you tell us about your money story?

I think it starts way back when my parents were dairy farmers and we had nine years of drought, so we had little-to-no money. I have two brothers, but we were pretty shielded because every day we had bacon and eggs for breakfast and meat and veg for dinner, which is what rich people eat, right? We didn't realise that, in fact, we were poor, because we grew it all on the farm.

When I was in Year 7, my mum worked in the school canteen so I helped her and got paid in snacks. That was my first job, I guess. From there I was like, if I work, I get things I like! So as soon I could, I got a job working for my nan in her catering business, then at Subway three days a week after school. When I left school I had a traineeship and worked a second job, then got a new job and still worked a second job. Up until 12 months ago, I've always had a second job.

Why is that?

I feel like my primary job is where I make money and my second job is what I enjoy; it's what I want to do. But I also get to make money while I'm doing it.

Do you ever get burnt out?

Not really. When I was younger, I worked in the catering business, I worked at Subway, I was a house sitter, I was a pet sitter. I'd work five jobs in three days and I just loved it. What else do you do? I didn't really have a social life, so I decided I was just going to go to work.

Love it. What was your traineeship in?

When I left school I was a trainee dental assistant. Growing up I'd always just wanted to get married and have kids, so I never had any ambitions about a career or university, but I did want to earn an income. A family friend owned the local dentist practice and I approached them for a job and they said yes. I left halfway through Year 12. It was a great job, but the people I worked with were not that great. The dentists were amazing, but I was 17 or 18, and a lot of the girls I worked with were in their mid-twenties and a bit on the bitchy side.

So after that, I went back into hospitality and worked at a dessert bar. By this time, I was with my partner. He was doing full-time shift work while I was working and running the household as well. I ended up working 50 hours a week and, with looking after the house and doing a second job, it was just way too much. So I swapped to a part-time job at a doctor's surgery for 20 hours a week.

Not long after, my partner had this bright idea to buy a coffee van; he wanted the tax write-offs and to build a franchise. Knowing that I love hospitality, I love coffee, I love people, he asked me to work for him. Initially, I tried to work my part-time job and the coffee van as well, but the coffee van just took off. Because we live in a mining town and my nan had a well-known catering business, I piggybacked off her and we got a lot of business very, very quickly. I was doing it full-time, getting up at 3 am every day for the business run and then on weekends we'd have an event every Saturday, every Sunday, and sometimes during the week too.

How much money was the business earning at that point?

Couldn't tell you. But when I was younger, my mum had a coffee van as well. The profit from that was insane. It cost 30 cents a coffee for the beans and the milk. And you charge a lot more!

So my partner and I made margins with the coffee cart, but it was a new business so we had to invest a bit and I wasn't getting paid. We had separate finances and I think I had $8000 in savings and it dwindled extremely quickly. I ran the household, I did the shopping and that obviously adds up. In the end I told him that the business needed to start paying me. But he didn't want to, and he didn't want to employ anyone else either. So I put my foot down and said it wasn't working. And that was the end of that.

The end of the coffee business or the end of the relationship?

Both, in the end. My partner really directed our relationship and our pathways, which at the time I was fine with; I was going to get married and have babies. But then I got diagnosed with endometriosis at age 19 and I realised that if I wasn't going to have kids, this wasn't the life I wanted.

I think I was so clouded by the fact that I wanted kids that I didn't really pay attention to the way things were going. But when I wasn't getting paid, I thought: I don't actually want to do this. I don't want this life that you're planning for us. Can we do something else? And he didn't want that.

But the coffee van ended, so I went and managed a local café for a bit, which didn't go well. The owners were underpaying everyone. I ended up taking it to Fair Trading and got $6500 back, which was a lot of money in 2016. I was only there for four months.

Around then, I put in for a dump truck traineeship, which is the job I do now. I didn't have a job offer, but I got so sick of not being paid that I ended up just quitting my job without anything to go to. And my partner did not like that. There were other things going on in the relationship, but my eyes were suddenly opened. I loved him, but I didn't want that life anymore. Heading off to night shift one night he called me lazy and unmotivated because I hadn't washed his work clothes and I hadn't cooked him dinner.

So I called my dad and he was there quick smart with his ute and horse float. I packed all my stuff and left.

How much were you earning at that point and how did you make ends meet?

I had the part-time dump truck traineeship and my wage worked out to be $500 a week, take home. I lived with my mum and her partner for four weeks, then moved into a rental which my cousins owned for about $250 a week. At various stages, I got flatmates, then mum moved in for a bit, and then I got my own place again. I worked so much overtime – I was picking up odd jobs, house sitting and pet sitting just to make ends meet. I knew I was in a shit situation, but that no-one could fix it for me. I just kept chugging along and watching my budget and eating really cheaply, not having a social life, not really doing anything, just going to the gym and going home.

Once the traineeship finished – altogether it took about two years – I began earning around $100,000, driving for the mines. I'd just turned 24 and having been diagnosed with endo and polycystic ovarian syndrome, I knew I probably wasn't going to have kids, so I joined Fire and Rescue New South Wales. I have so much to give, so much energy that I needed to do something else, have an outlet. Meanwhile, I still was doing my primary job.

On top of my trucker's wage I got paid between $15,000 and $25,000 a year as a firefighter, depending on how much I worked. I was the only female firefighter in a crew of 16. I grew up on a farm with two brothers so I don't mind getting my hands dirty, but when your pager goes off, you have to go down to the station in your normal clothes and then get changed into your uniform. The first couple of times the boys didn't know where to look, but I didn't care, I had underwear on!

In September 2020, just before I turned 25, I bought my first house. It was little, I couldn't afford a big family home so decided to use it as a stepping stone. Paying a mortgage back then was almost cheaper than renting and I had so much extra cash coming I was saving a lot really quickly, so in March 2021 I put a deposit on a block of land as well.

I was living with my boyfriend at the time, a deadbeat, unfortunately – I know I can pick them! We weren't even dating very long when he ended up in a pickle with his housing. His housemate was moving out and his lease was ending, so I let him move in. He really wanted to go in with me on the block of land, but we were new and I didn't feel comfortable. I told him I wanted it to be my financial responsibility, so if something ever happened, it was clearly mine. It was a good move, because we split up in the end and things got a bit ugly.

She's on the Money

When buying property together, even if you think you're in love and it will last forever and you're determined to buy together, it's best to have talked it all out and agreed upon what might happen in every potential scenario.

While there's a lot of debate around whether prenups and other similar agreements hold much weight in Australia, nonetheless, they show intent and, at the very least, force you to have the hard chat. I always say that if you're taking on what might be the biggest debt and responsibility of your life, then you should be able to talk through these difficult scenarios too.

Okay, so you're all happily sorted and single in your new house now?

Um, no, not quite. Soon after that, my best friend at the time, who's now my husband, bought a house in the same town as me. As we were both living alone during COVID, we created a family bubble. With my block of land getting closer to settling, the original plan had been that I would move in with my mum and rent out my current property so I didn't have to pay the two mortgages. But then my brother moved home, so I ended up moving in with Tom, my now husband, and we rented out my first property.

But then in October 2022, that house burnt down!

What?!

It was my day off, so I was working for the fire brigade, and a page came through at around 7 am saying there was a house fire. I was in bed and rolled over to Tom and told him I had to go and that I'd be a couple of hours. I went to the station, got on the truck and then asked the others where we were going. They told me but I was on autopilot and I didn't even know it was my house until we got there.

When we arrived I looked at my captain and told him it was my house. I was in hysterics and phoned Tom. He showed up a little while later and I just sat in the gutter and watched my house burn down.

The tenants had some batteries on charge in the shed and they must have overheated and combusted. The fire very quickly spread to the rest of the house.

That is so awful, I hope you're okay? How has it affected you, emotionally and financially?

I don't think I went to work for a whole week. But I'm a firefighter so I just had to keep on keeping on. The worst thing was, Tom and I were secretly engaged and had started planning our wedding. We'd even put down a deposit. But then the house burnt down and, even though we had landlord insurance, we lost the rental income which had been covering my mortgage repayments.

The house has now been demolished and we're waiting to rebuild. We just got council approval. But it's taken a year. We have a construction loan, which is stepped, so we only have to pay the interest on whatever stage the build is up to. But the place burnt down in October 2022 and our house was due to start being built in February 2023, so the payments started to rise. At one point, because our insurance money had stopped, we were paying three mortgages from our own paycheques. Thankfully my husband who's a boilermaker also earns decent money – $140,000 including super.

In August 2023, we eloped. When we came back, our house was ready but we were then paying the full mortgage. So we moved into our brand-new house and sold my husband's place for a nice little profit. Now that his house has been sold we currently just have the house we're in, which we pay a mortgage on, and then we're also paying the mortgage on the burnt-down investment property.

Gosh, so what's going on with that property now?

As with most landlord's insurance, rental income is covered for 12 months or until rectified, whichever comes first. It took way longer than that. They wouldn't demolish my house because it was insured for $430,000. My demolition allowance is 10 per cent, so $43,000, but they said it would cost $54,000. I didn't have any choice but to demolish it, so that cost me $18,000 out-of-pocket. Now they're saying they have to rebuild it from the slab up. So that's where we are currently on that.

And the new house we're in now also needs a lot more money. We chose a pretty basic package; no flooring, no driveways. As the loan was only in my name, it was hard to get much more than $1.2 million. It was very hard for a single female, but I did it. The deposit for my house and land in total was $94,000. By the time we finish our landscaping, the shed and our window furnishings, we'll have put $193,000 of our own cash into it.

That's so much money. And you've saved all of this?

A lot of it came from Tom's house sale. We actually have joint finances now. I run the ship, he just puts his money in there.

Two years ago I got a permanent position with the mine site, which means I got a massive pay rise. My gross wage including super and bonuses last year was $172,000. I'm very proud. I've worked a lot and I've done a lot, especially being a female. It's very hard out there.

And what's the plan for the future?

I want babies! Financially we could swing it, but when I was 21, my gynaecologist told me I may not be able to have kids because of the endo. He suggested we try before I'm 25 or, if that was too early for me to consider becoming a parent, we could look at freezing my eggs. So hopefully once the house gets rebuilt, we'll start.

You'll be so much more financially free once that's not a burden.

Yeah, but I am fully aware that I probably can't get pregnant, which is okay. We have two beautiful nieces and another one on the way.

And are you still a firefighter?

I actually resigned in April this year. I was moving a town over so I wouldn't get to stay in that station anyway. We fought fires and did rescue operations, whereas the one that I'm at now is very medical-based and not really my thing.

Apart from managing your properties, do you have any other big money goals you're working towards?

We want to buy a second investment property, but that will happen after the other one is built. We've also got a little cash hub from the profits from my husband's house sale.

And any other investments?

We just started seeing a financial advisor in June. I have super, which is just under $80,000. And then we have shares, just under $4500, and some bonds which are about $4500 too.

And what about debts, is it just the mortgages?

Yes, just the mortgages. Our investment property currently sits at $340,000 and our primary residence is $588,000.

And what's your best money habit?

Up until about 18 months ago, before I started earning more, I had never experienced lifestyle creep. But I've always been a really good saver. Whenever I'm shopping for furniture and other stuff for the new house, I will not buy anything unless it's on sale.

And your worst?

I love food and I have no shame about spending big on it. All of my spending goes on food. But my worst money habit is I'm so focused on future me that I sometimes forget to live my life now and be good to current me. I'm trying to find a balance and my husband has been helping me with that. So yeah, I'm trying to bring the focus back a little bit to right now and enjoying life. I'm only 28, after all!

So you're earning $180,000, you own all these properties, you've literally done so much stuff and you think you're a B plus. Are you pulling our leg?

No, I think I'm a B plus.

Why?

Well, KFC is too close to my house. And we did just drop $40,000 on a motorbike!

But that's within the budget?

It is. And I guess it's about trying to focus on current me, not future me. So maybe I'm an A minus.

From Bankruptcy to Building Solid Foundations

This money diarist was 16 when her parents went bankrupt. They lost everything and, as you can imagine, it had a profound effect on her. Fast forward to now, aged 24, she and her partner are engaged and are building their own house, but she just can't shake that nagging feeling that one day they might lose it all too . . .

Tell us a little bit about your money story.

The earliest memories I have are of my parents living paycheque to paycheque. They had their own business and worked really long hours, but it was very hard for them. We frequently heard that they had no money and it was a really big stressor.

When I was 16, their business went into involuntary administration, which sent us bankrupt and we lost everything, including our house and car. It was really brutal and it gave me a really negative perception of money. I genuinely felt like there was no way I'd ever be comfortable in life knowing that they had worked so hard yet got nothing out of it.

Around mid-last year I started reading some She's on the Money posts and felt like I was missing a lot of key information. So I went back and listened to every single podcast. I did a whole budget overhaul and it felt like I was getting myself into a much better position – I even started helping my partner with his financial literacy as he had also grown up in a low-income household.

Unfortunately though, we had a little hiccup earlier this year when my dad got very sick and ended up in a coma, but he's all good now. That put me in a bit of a rut, and I feel like I haven't quite gotten back on track yet.

You're on your way. What do you do for work and how much money do you earn?

I work in recruitment and my annual salary is $52,000 plus super. That brings in about $1600 a fortnight. However, all of my finances are shared with my fiancé who brings in around $1800 a fortnight too.

That's a good income. What's your big money goal? What are you currently working towards?

I kind of have three goals on the go. My major one is our emergency fund. We really need to build that up and it's something we're working really hard on. My fiancé and I are also building a house, so we're trying to save up to furnish it.

Congrats. You have a lot going on! How did your partner propose?

I thought I was surprising him by buying him the puppy of his dreams. He's always wanted a Bernese mountain dog. So we were driving there to pick up the dog but he took a wrong turn. Turns out my best friends had told him what was happening, so instead, he showed up with a giant box with a bell on it and the puppy and the ring were inside. It was beautiful and the most exciting thing ever and I bawl my eyes out every time I think about it.

So you didn't know the proposal was coming at all?

I had no inkling, which shocked me to the core because my partner cannot keep a secret to save his life!

How did he pay for the ring?

All of our funds are shared, which is why I didn't see it coming. He had asked me one week if he could help his parents out with their rent and I agreed. So he took about $300 out of our savings account for the deposit but described it as 'rent'. The ring was being custom made so he didn't have to pay the last part until it was finished. At that point he reached out to my best friend and asked if she'd pay the balance and he'd pay her back so I wouldn't see the money coming out of our account. She paid for it and then as soon as he proposed we just transferred the money back to her. So I didn't see it coming at all!

Love it! He sounds amazing. Can you tell us how you're helping him lift his level of financial literacy?

The very first time I approached him about helping him learn something, it was actually investment related. He was a little apprehensive at the start, and he definitely knew more than I did before I began listening to the *She's on the Money* podcast. But I sent him a podcast link and said, I want you to look at it the same way that I'm looking at it and teach me what I'm missing. So we came at it as a team and brainstormed it.

Brilliant! You guys are wizards!

He's very smart and very receptive – totally open to learning more if it's going to put us in a better position. Once I explained that I was listening to the podcast because I want us to be in a good spot, to invest and to understand money and how it all works, he was totally on board.

Okay, great! So, do you have any investments?

Aside from my superannuation, no. But I really want to invest, especially after listening to the podcast. I always thought investing was just a dream for rich people who knew what they were doing with their money. I didn't think that it would ever be possible for me. Our focus is getting our emergency savings set up first and then the investing will come after.

That's the plan, that's how it works. You're building a strong financial house. Do you have any debts?

We're obviously building the house, so we have a building loan for that. Each progress stage adds more to the loan and it will be a $500,000 loan once construction's complete. At the moment we're just doing interest-only repayments. We also have a joint car loan which we're trying to get rid of, and that's sitting at $27,000 at the moment for our two cars.

What's your best money habit?

A great habit that I learnt from *She's on the Money* was to put time between me and my purchases. So that's my best money habit for sure.

And what about your worst money habit?

I'm horrible at sticking to a budget when it comes to buying things for my family and friends. Gift giving is my love language. I love to spoil my friends and family, so I set myself a budget, but never actually stick to it.

If we forced you to give yourself a grade when it came to your money habits, what would you grade yourself?

I'd say a C. That's where I'm at right now.

What makes up that C and what would it take to improve it?

Building up our emergency fund. Since my dad got sick I went totally off track, so I need to redo my budget and cashflow. I just keep putting it off because it stresses me out. But once that's back in place, it would take my grade a bit higher. Investing would probably get me to an A.

Do you have a goal number in mind for your emergency fund?

Right now we're aiming for around $10,000. It feels like a safe amount. We have two dogs and want enough in our emergency fund to cover the costs if they have any emergency vet visits.

Tell us a bit more about how your parents' bankruptcy impacted your relationship with money.

It really put a dampener on everything. And it was definitely at the back of my mind when we were buying our house. Our mortgage broker kept reiterating that we had enough to service the loan and that we'd be okay, but until we got the piece of paper in the mail that said we'd been approved, I kept thinking it wouldn't go through. My parents are such hard workers. My dad was working 80-hour weeks, so to have had everything just ripped from their hands makes me feel like it's hard to get ahead.

My partner and I took out a personal loan for our two cars because there's no public transport where I live. But the cars are really unreliable and we just keep spending money on them; a thousand here, a thousand there. But we need them and being able to commit to that and say, yeah, I'm willing to go into debt to get them was so difficult for me because I felt like it was just going to start the whole process of us ending up where my parents were.

That must be so hard because you obviously want to put yourself ahead financially and make good decisions, but at the same time it's always in the back of your mind. But you two, you're just starting out and you have the chance to entirely rewrite your money story! Have you discussed the wedding budget yet?

Very vaguely. I just don't know how much a wedding costs and I don't want to set an unrealistic budget. I'm in the process of researching venues and other things we really want as a part of our wedding and how much all of that is going to cost.

So you're having good, open, honest conversations about it and are on the same page?

We're pretty good at being on the same page with these sorts of things. We're doing the research together and discussing what's important for me and what's super important for my fiancé to get to the finer details of what we have to have and what is negotiable to make a budget work. We don't want to throw out a random figure and say, this is our budget, and then have to keep going over it because we haven't researched it properly.

Weddings are expensive and it's pretty stressful. There's definitely a ton of things that I never would've even considered, but I'm lucky that we've got a very good friend who married recently, so she's helping me.

That's great you've got someone like that on your team. But back to your money goals. How did you figure out how to prioritise which of those goals you want to achieve and how much money you're allocating?

I sat down and said, okay, these are the things we need to work on. Let's just make sure that they're all happening.

I think the emergency fund is our top priority. We're lucky, in that the work that my partner and I do was quite stable throughout COVID. I know we were really privileged with that, whereas it was very hard for a lot of people. We've managed to work a bit on the emergency fund and that's reassuring in case something happens to our dogs or our cars.

The next priorities are the house and the wedding. It'd be horrible if we had to push the wedding back, but if we have to it won't be the end of the world. We put the house as our middle priority because it's going to come up sooner than the wedding and we're going to need a bed, a couch, a fridge and all those sorts of things.

Those basics all add up and can start to feel overwhelming. But planning ahead is the best way to get there. In terms of building your house, how did that come about and why did you decide to build rather than buy something established?

As I say, my partner came from a low-income household and I came from a very rocky financial household, so neither of us had ever lived in a brand-new house. We'd never had all those exciting new finishes that most people dream of, that had never been a thing in either of our lives. Also, the market for established houses was sky high. But the major kicker was definitely that we wanted something that was brand new, where everything we picked would be perfect for us, compared to something that had been built for someone else which we'd have to fit into.

How did you find the process of picking everything out? Did any upgrades eat into your budget?

We really enjoyed the process. We were told to expect to spend about $30,000 extra on upgrades. That includes things like your air conditioning, your flooring, everything like that which weren't included in our base quote. We actually came in about $10,000 under, so we ended up spending about $20,000 on the extras. We also picked a builder who provided a lot of good standard inclusions because some of them don't, so you're forced to pay for a lot of upgrades. Designing and picking all the finishes for the home was the most exciting part.

She's on the Money

Off-the-plan purchases and house-and-land packages give you access to the construction company's buying power as well as a construction loan arrangement.

In these arrangements you pay the loan in installments as the build progresses, reaching the total cost once the building is complete. As you're choosing the finishes, you also get more of a say on the end result, both of which may offer a degree of flexibility that buying an existing property doesn't.

Be aware, though, that you're buying 'sight unseen', even if you've taken a peek at the show homes. In reality, your finishes may not compare with what you'd imagined and there's always some degree of risk until the building is finished. In recent years we've seen many building companies go into administration.

Whichever path you choose, make sure you've done your research so you can feel confident in the choice you make.

How brilliant that you're building your own home. Did you ever think that that was going to become the reality for you?

Never. Not even in my wildest dreams. I always felt like if I'm not working the 80 hours my dad did, how would I ever have a chance? I thought it was never going to happen for us. My partner wasn't earning a lot of money when we first got together eight years ago. I was 14, he was 16, we both worked at Maccas and that wasn't going to set us up to build a house and to be where we are right now. But we've done it and I'm proud of us!

A Hard Start to Now Flipping the Script!

This money diarist came from a single-parent home where she became a young carer and experienced financial trauma, yet she's flipped her life around. She wants people to know that if you keep working hard, eventually the seeds you plant will fruit. Now 27 and happily single, she runs her own business and, after 18 months, has only $80,000 left on her mortgage.

First question, can you tell us a little bit about your money story?

I was just finishing primary school when my parents announced that they were getting a divorce. Money had always been tight – there'd always been arguments over it – but after that it became worse. I was 12, and felt constantly unsettled, stressed, sad and kind of helpless. It took about two years for my parents' divorce to settle. After that, Mum could buy a family home, but it came with really high interest rates and high repayments, which were hard for her to maintain as a single parent.

It put a lot of pressure on Mum's shoulders to be both parents and sole provider. Ultimately, it was too overwhelming for her, so she basically gave up and I stepped in and took over. We sought out a mortgage broker and, at the age of 14, I learnt very quickly about interest rates, deposits, equity, offset accounts, terms and conditions, various lenders, house valuations, credit scores, and all the rest. Mum's situation was pretty complex, so it took around nine months to sort out, but I successfully refinanced the family home, which is kinda crazy to look back on. From then on, I was very finance focused.

Through school, I worked in retail and used my savings to build Mum's emergency fund. Then, throughout university, I kept a part-time job to assist with my family's financial situation and keep a roof over our heads. But it did affect my mental health as I would work weekends to get maximum pay which prevented me from having any kind of social life. As time went on and the kids grew up, things got more and more expensive and the family situation worsened. I often thought about dropping out of uni so I could help more, but in the end, decided to keep going. I hoped that eventually my education would pay off.

I graduated from university and got a job as a therapist. However, as with many first jobs, the conditions were pretty poor. My mental health declined further, but the pay was good, so I kept at it. I was just so driven to get increasingly better jobs for higher pay, regardless of what the conditions were like. Numerous burnouts later, I decided: this is enough, I need to flip the script. I need to stop my story from being so negative and make it something positive.

My first decision was to use money to bring happiness and joy. Because I was in my early twenties, my idea was to travel . . . but COVID popped that dream, so I turned to property, which I knew through and through. In 2020, I bought my first apartment: a two-by-one with a view of the river. I took the 'worst house on the best street' approach and spent months renovating it, saving for each stage and doing as much as I could myself while spending all my money on it. I wanted to get some profit back after I'd finished, so I put it on Airbnb and, to my surprise, it took off. Now I full-time Airbnb it to help with my mortgage.

I also decided to change my employment story, so I switched jobs and cut my hours. Instead of getting another job and repeating the cycle, I decided to start my own business, putting my mental health and work–life balance first. I also stepped away, financially, from my family. I felt they were in a good enough spot. So right now, I have a very positive attitude towards money and I'm finally reaping the fruit of the seeds I've sown.

Oh my gosh, what a journey. You said you flipped your employment script. What do you do for work? How much money do you earn?

I am a therapist in the NDIS realm and earn about $185,000 a year. While people might think that's unusual for a carer, I have seven-plus years' experience under my belt and also work very, very hard. I do a lot of hours because the work keeps coming in and I keep accepting it. The NDIS rate is very good and I don't have any overheads. I'm mobile, so I just go straight to my clients' houses and I don't have any bosses or employees, just my bookkeeper. So I can charge the full rate and keep pretty much all of it.

Talk to me, what is your big money goal? It sounds like you've done a lot already.

My big money goal is to create several streams of passive income by earning rental income on numerous properties, dividends from shares, interest earnings on saving accounts – whatever means possible.

Awesome. So tell us, do you have any investments?

Obviously, my apartment is my biggest investment. I've had some shares since I was 15 that pay me dividends each six months, which is great, and a bit of crypto. I don't feel educated enough in that realm, so I just put my toe in. I also get interest from various savings accounts. I'd like to think they're a form of investment too.

People often complain about not getting good rates of return on their savings accounts. What are you using? Are you getting good rates of return at this point in time?

It depends how you look at it. In my previous retail jobs I used to earn $20 an hour. So now when I get $20 of interest I'm like, that's a whole hour's pay! I see interest more like free money than earnings.

I love that. Alright, I know you've got a mortgage, but do you have any other debts?

My mortgage is my 'good debt'. My 'okay debt' is my student loan which should be paid off by next year. And that's basically it; everything else has been paid off in full.

You said you had $80,000 left on your mortgage. How much did you buy for and how quickly have you smashed that down?

The interesting story with my house is that originally they wanted $300,000 for it. But then COVID hit and no-one was buying and the house market was absolutely crashing. So then they wanted $250,000. I negotiated it down to $183,000.

Money win! That's epic, tell us more.

I think I was really lucky. I did go for another apartment, but that fell through and I was pretty bummed about it. So I realised I had to act quite quickly if I wanted something.

I said to Mum, come with me, let's have a look at this one, see what you think and we'll go from there. We walked in at three o'clock on a Wednesday afternoon and by five o'clock, I'd bought it. It was one of those crazy things that was just meant to be.

The realtor was like, look, there's someone else looking at this property as well. If you're serious about it, please put an offer in. The owner had held it for about 25 years and she just wanted it to go to a good home. The realtor told her, she comes from a good family and she's worked really hard and has a big deposit.

Initially I offered $181,000, but the vendor had her heart set on $185,000 minimum. I countered with $183,000 and she accepted. She wrote me a letter wishing me all the best and to have good times there. So it wasn't a profit thing for her, more about finding the right person to give them a good start in life.

I had a 20 per cent deposit, so my mortgage was $146,400. I've paid off $60,000 or so.

Queen! Next question, what is your best money habit?

My best money habit is that I save for everything. Everything I've bought, I saved for beforehand so I could pay in full. All my renos I saved for and did as I could afford them. It was the same with wanting a car. I was like, right, I have to save for it first and then pay for it in full.

To flip that on its head, what's your worst money habit?

I focus too much on 'the want': I *want* to save this much money a week rather than I *can* save this much money a week, which puts me under too much pressure. I tell myself I want to save $200 but find I can't because I've got big bills coming in. I get really stressed which confuses everything and makes my everyday budgeting really murky. I need to be more realistic.

And what grade would you give your money habits?

Probably a B plus, because my everyday budgeting is not super clear, realistic or automated. I would like to clean it up to decrease the stress I have around finance.

Back to your family circumstances – at age 14, you became the one dealing directly with a mortgage broker to re-finance your family home. Why do you think you ended up being the driving force?

It's a good question. I do have an older brother and two younger brothers, but I think, when it came to responsibility, it fell on my shoulders because my parents knew I was financially driven and had taught myself the basic things: how to save, what interest was, et cetera. When I learnt about compound interest, I was like, what is this magic?! So when push came to shove and I saw Mum not coping I felt that although I had no idea what I was doing, I had no choice but to give it a go.

Luckily, we had a really good mortgage broker who identified the situation and could see what was happening. He was aware that my older brother was not at all savvy with money, so he looked at me and decided: this person knows what she's doing, I'll walk her through it. I'd run down and get Mum's signature, then come back and get the next instruction. When Mum was ill, I was the one taking her to hospital and medical appointments and keeping the family running. So I think, because I had that responsibility on my shoulders, the financial stuff just fell into my lap too. I also think there's a part of me that just wants to fix everything and save everyone, for my family's sake.

That sounds like a really big burden to carry. Are you okay now with that? How do you feel when we reflect on that?

Initially, I felt quite emotional – I'd almost forgotten I'd done all that; in a weird way, I'd kind of normalised it all. When I was looking for an apartment I brought a ton of experience so I knew what I was doing, but then I'd talk to my friends who had no clue where to start which I found really strange. But then I realised, oh, *that's* why you have that knowledge and *that's* how your experience has shaped you. I guess I'm very determined about using hard experiences as a way to flourish. Like, okay, this horrible situation happened to you, you were forced to step into a kind of co-parenting role and have adult responsibilities, but now, let's try and use that to your advantage.

I have to always remind myself, you did that, you're amazing, that's incredible! Now I'm getting older, I'm making sure that I appreciate and look after myself more. Part of that, with the help of your podcast, was identifying that I probably do carry some financial trauma; that what I went through was not your typical 12-year-old life, and now, I'm working through that.

I do get psychological help to unpack it. It's interesting because I have a love–hate relationship with money: I love earning it and building it and using it to travel and to build my investments and things like that, but then there's also this trauma around, do I have enough of it? Am I working hard enough? Is it all going to blow up tomorrow, sort of thing.

It's still a work in progress, but I'm definitely doing a lot better and just taking those mental breaks when I need them. I try to be kind to myself, like, okay, maybe don't check the mortgage numbers today and don't panic so much about only having this much in your savings. I'm really working at putting better boundaries around finance.

She's *on the* Money

Financial trauma is a chronic mental health condition that develops in response to a traumatic event or period surrounding money, such as growing up in poverty, being financially abused, or suddenly being confronted with loss.

Where financial stress is short-term anxiety over a current situation, financial trauma is long-term and changes the way we think, feel and behave. Signs include: compulsive over- or under-spending, a lack of financial boundaries, workaholism, a scarcity mindset, avoidance, excessive risk aversion or conversely, reckless behaviour.

As it can be quite complex to identify and resolve, working with mental health professionals can be really helpful if this is something you've identified that you might be struggling with.

Was that a jarring moment when you realised, wait, no, that was a traumatic circumstance as opposed to 'just how you grew up'?

Yeah, it was a slow dawning. I'd kind of flagged financial trauma a couple months before I heard your podcast, then when I heard your podcast I was like, tick, tick, tick, me, me, me. Initially, when you look back on your behaviour you think, oh, that's just me, nothing unusual here. But then you unpack it a bit and you're like, actually no, there's a reason why I have a bookkeeper and don't want to know anything about the financials. I'm very much, yep, you guys sort it – just tell me how much tax to pay.

I've become very big on figuring out why things are making me feel the way I'm feeling. I have anxiety and have been battling and managing that for many, many years and I think that's what came first. I've always struggled, but it reached breaking point when I kept questioning whether I should stay on at uni or drop out and go full-time in retail to help my family's financial situation. I was being torn in two. What do I do? Do I help myself, or help my family? I felt really uncomfortable about letting my family down, but also with supporting my dreams. So I started getting psychological help.

My anxiety had grown into what's termed generalised anxiety, which means that it's not triggered by a particular situation, but that you're in a persistent state of anxiety all the time. It was a lightbulb moment when I realised that this was very much built around my anxiety towards finance because of not having a lot of it growing up and it being used to control and manipulate my circumstances.

I was permanently carrying this thought: if you don't have it, you're going to lose everything – your house, your this, that and the other. So I was always working so hard to make sure I had more than enough. When I realised I was carrying this fear, it was upsetting at first because no-one likes to have trauma in their life, but then it became, right, how do I unpack this? How do I grow from this? I can't undo the past, but I can change the future. How do I manage this and use it as a strength?

I think that's so important. What would you say to those who are going through similar circumstances?

Reaching out for help was the hardest thing for me to do; it took me a long time to admit I needed it. Given the family situation I was in and being the one they all relied on, I never felt like I could not be okay. So it took me a long time to acknowledge that I was struggling and to pick up the phone and call a counsellor. I'm glad I eventually did. Once I had, I became more comfortable with asking for help and expressing my feelings. Being a therapist, I've since become very good at communicating, this is how I'm feeling, this is what I'm doing. I've started to normalise that between my friends too, so we say, hey, this is how I'm feeling today; hey, this is what's going on; hey, this is where my head's at.

For anyone who's in a similar situation, I say, prioritise your mental health. There have been times where I was so financially focused I kept working these jobs with rubbish conditions, finding myself shaking all the time and having panic attacks, but telling myself, don't worry it'll pay off because you'll get a bigger salary in the next job. Looking back, I wish I'd had a bit more patience and just been like, okay, you need to just stop and look after your mental health. That although it might take another six months or year to get where you want to be financially, that's not the important thing. The important thing is your wellbeing.

The *most* important thing is to feel okay when you wake up in the morning; to feel happy and not carry that heavy chest feeling. That's the most valuable thing and that should always be your focus. It's a matter of reaching out for help and also re-evaluating what's important to you. Valuing finance is super important, but valuing your mental wellbeing will get you everywhere. Finance is a long-term game, not short-term. As much as you might be going through hardship, you've got to play the long game.

PROPERTY JOURNALLING PROMPTS

How does thinking about money and property ownership make you feel? Why do you think that is – what stories and beliefs have you inherited from your upbringing?

If you are dreaming of owning property, write out a plan for how you might realistically get there, listing major milestones and dates.

If you are thinking about going into property with someone else, it's important you're on the same page. Write out your specific goals: what's important to you emotionally and financially and how you're going to pay it off.

We all have more power than we realise to change certain situations in our lives. What's one area of your life where you'd like to flip the script? Why is it so important to you to create change in that area? How will you feel when you've flipped that script?'

Property Money Wins

LEESA worked with her mortgage broker a year after she settled on the purchase of her home to ensure she was getting the best deal. She was able to get a discount on her current loan from the new loan provider and will save approximately $4000 a year with the new loan!

JAZ is doing some kitchen renovations and landed some kitchen cabinets for $140 off Facebook Marketplace, score! After more research, she even found a cheaper alternative to create the benchtops she wants, and it will only cost $200 for the supplies instead of over $3000!

ANNIE listed her home for sale and her agent suggested she pay $2000 for it to be staged. Instead, Annie decided to pick up some free home décor items on Facebook Marketplace and through community groups. She also purchased some additional furniture pieces from op shops and Kmart. In total, she spent around $500 and kept some of the new furniture for her new house. So much better than paying a stylist and renting furniture that you don't get to keep!

IMOGEN is building a new house and shopped around for quotes to construct two gates near the front entrance of the property. The first contractor said it would be $1760 for the two gates. She got a second quote for one gate and they advised it would only be an extra $300 for the other gate. She saved $1070!

ASHLEIGH scored some IKEA drawers in near new condition on Facebook Marketplace for $100 instead of $699 brand new. Bonus – she doesn't have to put them together!

HANNAH normally gets anxious about making phone calls, but she worked up the courage to call her bank to see if they could reduce her home loan rate. She wasn't happy with the deal, so she held her ground and requested a discharge form and contacted her mortgage broker. She is now in the process of applying for a much better rate which will save her thousands in the long run!

SARAH'S rent was raised $90 but she negotiated with her landlord and haggled it down to just a $50 increase. Every dollar counts!

RACHEL is renovating the shelving in her unit and is saving $400 by removing the old shelves herself. Demolition mode pays off!

NICOLA got in touch with an insurance broker after her home insurance came up for renewal. She is now paying less per month than she did last year.

SENNA worked two jobs and closed her buy now, pay later accounts in less than four months, so she could start saving for a house deposit. She says listening to SOTM has been essential in helping her focus on her home-buying goals!

YOUR MONEY DIARY

Throughout this book, you've worked through a series of journalling prompts. Now that you've read the stories from our community, if I were interviewing you as a money diarist, how might you answer these standard Money Diary questions?

What's your attitude towards money?

....

....

....

What do you for work and how much do you earn?

....

....

....

What's your big money goal?

....

....

....

Do you have investments?

....

....

....

Do you have debts?

....

....

....

What is your best money habit?

....

....

....

What is your worst money habit?

....

....

....

Now that you've read through this book and answered the journalling prompts, what grade would you give your money habits from A to F?

....

....

....

CONNECTING WITH YOUR MONEY STORY

This activity is from my first book *She's on the Money*, but because I think that understanding your money story is so crucial to creating success for your financial future, I've included it again here. If you've done this before, it might be an interesting process to do it again today and compare your answers to see how far you've come and what's still holding you back.

- What is the first thing that came to mind when the topic of money stories came up?
- How were finances handled in your family when you were growing up?
- Were financial expectations different for men and women? If so, what were the differences?
- What is your earliest memory about money?
- Was money spoken about as a family? If so, do you think those conversations impacted you in a positive way?
- Did anyone influence your money story in a positive way?

What are your money beliefs?

Beliefs are assumptions we hold to be true. When we use our beliefs to make decisions, we are assuming that the causal relationships of the past, which led to those beliefs being formed, will also apply in the future. In a rapidly changing world where complexity is increasing day by day, using information from the past to make decisions about the future may not be the best approach. Beliefs are contextual: they arise from learnt experiences, resulting from the cultural and environmental situations we have faced.

I want you to start thinking about your money beliefs and answer the questions below.

- Do you believe money is good or bad? Or is it just an evil necessity?

- Do you think money should be spent or saved?
- What would you consider a luxury purchase?
- Do you think money is hard or easy to obtain?
- Do you think money should be your responsibility, your partner's, or both?
- Do you think both parties in a relationship should be empowered to make financial decisions?
- Do you think money in a marriage should be separate or shared?
- Where do you think these beliefs came from?

What are your money values?

Your money values are different from your money beliefs. Values are not based on information from the past and they are not contextual. Values are intimately related to our needs. Whatever we need, whatever is important to us or whatever is missing from our lives – that is what we value. A good way to check what your values are is to check your bank statement and highlight what you spend most of your disposable income on. While you may think you value paying off your mortgage, your spending habits may reveal that you actually value nights out with friends more, and that's why you have so many pub and wine bar charges. As our life conditions change and as we mature and grow, our values change. When we use our values to make decisions, we focus on what is important to us or what we need in order to feel a sense of wellbeing.

What do you currently think you value?

....

....

Would you be willing to cut back on any of those activities or purchases?

- If yes, why? ....
- If no, why not? ....

Beliefs versus values

Being able to differentiate between your beliefs and your values will help you get your head in the right space to adjust your behaviour with money. Neuroplasticity refers to the ability to retrain your brain and change your habits. As much as your money story is defining your habits right now, you can absolutely change your trajectory.

Reflecting on your beliefs and values, how do they make you feel?

....

....

Are they aligned with creating the life you want for your future?

....

....

Are your beliefs getting in the way of your goals?

....

....

Reframe your thoughts

Most purchases are emotive. Have you ever had a really crappy day and thought, I deserve my favourite gelato right now, or, if I go and get that facial, I will feel much more confident at my work Christmas party, which will then help me network better and ultimately get me that new account? This is called retail therapy. It's your mind literally trying to soothe itself through shopping, and while it may hit the spot in the moment, it is detrimental to your bank account in the long run.

Another major cause of money anxiety is the unintentional practice of comparing yourself to others. When you talk to colleagues, friends or family members about salaries, savings, holidays, homes and the latest smart watch or phone, you can often end up feeling like you're not where you're supposed to be in life, which damages your sense of self-worth. It's important to know that the world is not a level playing field, and that we did not all start at the same point. Don't compare your start to someone else's middle.

Our minds constantly give us chatter and feedback, but sometimes these voices in our head can be negative and unhelpful. By learning to tune in to this chatter and reframe the messaging, you can consciously shift the tone to neutral or positive, which can lead to better decision-making in every area of your life. Over the years, I've learnt that people have excuses for everything. When people say, I can't, they usually mean, I won't make that a priority right now. It doesn't matter what salary you're on when you say you can't save. You would if it meant a lot to you. You're choosing not to achieve it (even if you don't realise it).

Financial independence is about mindset and approach. Since your emotions are guiding your purchasing decisions, you need to be able to reframe your reactions to your thoughts so that they align with your values.

Take one of the money beliefs you came up with earlier that has associated negative emotions for you. It might be a belief that makes you feel mad, sad, frustrated, stressed, trapped or worried.

Write down the thought that created this feeling, and how you usually act upon this belief.

....

....

How can you reframe this event in a way that will bring more positive emotions and less negative ones?

....

....

Support Resources

13 Yarn – 13 92 76

13yarn.org.au

13 Yarn is a national crisis support line for mob who are feeling overwhelmed or having difficulty coping. Confidential one-on-one yarning with a Lifeline-trained Aboriginal and Torres Strait Islander Crisis Supporter.

1800 RESPECT – 1800 737 732

1800respect.org.au

1800RESPECT is the national domestic, family and sexual violence counselling, information and support service.

ASIC Moneysmart

moneysmart.gov.au

A government-led information service provided by the Australian Securities and Investments Commission (ASIC), offering financial guidance for all Australians.

Beyond Blue – 1300 224 636

beyondblue.org.au

Support for Australians facing anxiety, depression and suicide.

Butterfly Foundation – 1800 334 673

butterfly.org.au

Butterfly Foundation is the national charity for all Australians impacted by eating disorders and body image issues, and for the families, friends and communities who support them.

Financial Information Service

servicesaustralia.gov.au/financial-information-service

A free government service that can inform and educate you about financial matters through online guides and talking to service officers.

HECS/HELP remissions

studyassist.gov.au/paying-back-your-loan/cancel-your-help-debt-under-special-circumstances

Information about eligibility criteria and how to apply for a remission of your HECS/HELP debt.

Lifeline – 13 11 14

lifeline.org.au

A national charity providing 24-hour crisis support and suicide prevention services.

Mob Strong Debt Helpline – 1800 808 488

financialrights.org.au/getting-help/mob-strong-debt-help

Free legal advice service about money matters for Aboriginal and Torres Strait Islander peoples from anywhere in Australia.

National Debt Helpline – 1800 007 007

ndh.org.au

Free advice on how to manage your debts, financial counselling and your financial rights.

Rural Financial Counselling Service (RFCS) – 1300 771 741

agriculture.gov.au/agriculture-land/farm-food-drought/drought/rural-financial-counselling-service

Free rural financial counselling for regional communities.

SANE – 1800 187 263

sane.org

Support services for people over 18 years of age with complex mental health needs, including people with intellectual disability, autism or acquired brain injury, and support for their family, friends and carers.

Small Business Help Debt Line – 1800 413 828

sbdh.org.au

Free financial counselling for small business owners and sole traders in financial difficulty.

Suicide Call Back Service – 1300 659 467

suicidecallbackservice.org.au

Free professional 24/7 counselling support for people at risk of or affected by suicide and for those experiencing emotional or mental health issues.

Acknowledgements

Congratulations, you've made it to the end! Having reached this point, I hope that the incredible stories so generously shared by our community have inspired you to rewrite your own money story. I'm equally excited to write these acknowledgements! They're one of my favourite parts of a book to write as I get to pour my heart out with gratitude for the people who have supported me in creating these pages. She's on the Money isn't a one-man band, it's a village.

To Stephen. In my first book I thanked you for being my partner, in my second book for being my fiancé, in my third book for being my husband and now in my fourth book I give you the most special thanks of all – for being the incredible dad you are to our son, Harvey. You truly are the best person I know. It is an absolute privilege to be married to you and now to have a family with you. Watching you become a dad has been one of the greatest joys of my life and I can't wait to continue on this adventure with you! You are generous, and kind, and the best human that Harvey could have as a role model. Thank you for always supporting me, no matter how wild my ideas! For that, I appreciate you more than you will ever know.

To my son, Harvey. I am so, so grateful I get to be your mum. You have brought me happiness and a love like I have never known before. Dream big and know you can accomplish anything you want in this world. I am so excited to watch you grow and will be by your side every step of the way.

To my parents, Judi and Eric Devine. Thank you for all that you have done for me and continue to do for me. I am forever grateful that I get to have parents like you who encouraged me to believe that I could achieve all my wildest dreams. The support, kindness and love you show to both Alex and me is incredible and I feel grateful every day for that. It has brought the biggest smile to my face watching you both become grandparents for the first time. Harvey is so lucky to have you both.

To Isabelle Yates – book number four, can you believe it?! You are the best publisher I could ask for. Thank you for your continuous support and patience as we go through this journey together. I couldn't do it without you and appreciate your love and guidance more than you know! And to Charle Malycon and Lydia Burgham, some more superstars on my Penguin team – your time and energy that goes into helping me create the perfect book for our readers is so admirable. I am beyond grateful I have you in my corner and it is a joy to work with you both. Penguin truly feels like home and I can't thank you all enough for the endless love and support. Here's to more books in the future, I say!

And as always, to *you*. You, my friends, are the very reason I wrote this book! This book is all about showcasing how incredible you all are. Words cannot describe how proud I am that you are a part of my community. This collection of stories shows us how money impacts everyone, irrespective of our background or where we've come from. We will all go through our own struggles and achievements on our financial journeys. I hope these pages allow you to see that you are not alone and that change is always possible.

This book is truly so special to me and I feel so honoured that I've had the privilege of hearing these stories. It is my hope that through reading these pages you have learnt that it is always possible to rewrite your money story and will use it to transform your future beliefs, actions and outcomes. Here's to future you!

She's
on the
Money
Take charge of your
financial future
Victoria Devine
Creator of Australia's #1 finance podcast

Winner of the ABIA General Non-fiction Book of the Year 2022

Winner of the Best Personal Finance & Investment Book of the Year at the 2021 Business Book Awards

Through her phenomenally popular and award-winning podcast **She's on the Money**, Victoria Devine has built an empowered and supportive community of women finding their way to financial freedom.

Honest, relatable, non-judgemental and motivating, Victoria is a financial adviser who knows what millennial life is really like and where we can get stuck with money stuff. (Did someone say 'Afterpay' . . . ?) So, to help you hit your money goals without skimping on brunch, she's put all her expert advice into this accessible guide that will set you up for a healthy and happy future.

Learn how to be more secure, independent and informed with your money – with clear steps on how to budget, clear debts, build savings, start investing, buy property and much more. And along with all the practical information, Victoria will guide you through the sometimes-tricky psychology surrounding money so you can establish the values, habits and confidence that will help you build your wealth long-term.

Just like the podcast, the book is full of real-life money stories from members of the **She's on the Money** community who candidly share their experiences, wins and lessons learned to inspire others to turn their stories around, too. And with templates and activities throughout, plus a twelve-month plan to get you started, you can immediately put Victoria's recommendations into action in your own life.

You are not alone on your financial journey, and with the money principles in this book you'll go further than you ever thought possible.

From the bestselling author of She's on the Money
Investing with
She's on the Money
Build your future wealth
Victoria Devine
Creator of Australia's #1 finance podcast

Shortlisted for ABIA General Non-fiction Book of the Year 2023

The ultimate millennial investment guide from the award-winning, number one bestselling author of **She's on the Money**.

Through the **She's on the Money** podcast and online community, and her bestselling first book, millennial financial adviser Victoria Devine has helped thousands of Australians take charge of their financial futures.

Investing is a huge part of building wealth, which is why Victoria's second book is all about learning how and why to invest and taking confident action to create an investment portfolio that will set you up for security and prosperity later in life.

Start by understanding your money mindset, risk profile and why you can't afford not to invest – especially if you're a woman (thanks, gender inequality!). Dive deep into the various ways you can invest in the stock market and learn more about property investment. Discover how your superannuation has already made you an investor and get the low-down on ethical investing before creating your own investment strategy that reflects your goals and values.

Covering all this and more, Victoria's straightforward guidance and practical activities in **Investing with She's on the Money** will have you feeling educated, empowered and ready to grow your future wealth in no time. Everyone has different starting points, but it's never too early or too late to begin your investing journey – so let's do this!

The ultimate first home buyer's guide
Property with She's on the Money
Victoria Devine
AWARD-WINNING AND BESTSELLING AUTHOR

Smash your property goals with Victoria Devine's informative guide – whether you're getting your first foot on the ladder, hunting for your dream home or planning for an investment property.

Even with the challenges involved (interest rates and crazy-high house prices, we're looking at you!), so many of us still really want to own property.

Whether it's the security and financial perks of owning your home or the benefits of having an investment property, the appeal and rewards are many.

But buying a property can also be one of the biggest decisions you'll ever make, so you want to get it right – right?

Luckily, Victoria Devine has written **Property with She's on the Money** to equip you for the whole process – from establishing your property values and truly understanding *why* you want to buy a home, to saving for the all-important deposit, which key experts to speak to, all things mortgages, what to buy and when, and how to make every stage of the process as smooth as possible – right through to renovating and selling.

It's packed with practical advice, innovative ideas and real-life stories from members of the **She's on the Money** community who have achieved their home ownership goals.

With this game-changing guide, property is no longer confusing, overwhelming and out-of-reach. It's clear, inspiring – and totally within your power.

She's *on the* Money

budget journal

Today is the day to change your financial future

Victoria Devine

Bestselling author of *She's on the Money*

Take charge of your financial future with this must-have guided journal from Victoria Devine, author of the award-winning bestseller **She's on the Money**.

If you've been inspired by the **She's on the Money** podcast and books to take positive action for your finances, then you're ready to meet your new best friend: **She's on the Money Budget Journal**.

Start at any time in the year and use it to:

- Map out your money with helpful tools and monthly budgets
- Set and stick to short-term and long-term money goals
- Track your daily expenses – as well as money wins and confessions
- Get organised and reduce stress come tax time
- Plan ahead to enjoy celebrations and festive seasons
- Keep all your financial notes, reflections and inspiration in one place
- Complete mini-challenges and supercharge your progress.

Every small step in your financial journey adds up. Using her financial training and experience to empower her clients and community, Victoria has designed this fun and practical guided journal to help you build the money habits that will help you reach your dreams.

Powered by Penguin